SOURCES FOR SOCIAL AND ECONOMIC HISTORY

Free Trade

SOURCES FOR SOCIAL AND ECONOMIC HISTORY

GENERAL EDITOR: *E. R. R. Green, Senior Lecturer in History, University of Manchester*

THE FACTORY SYSTEM   VOLUME I: BIRTH AND GROWTH
J. T. Ward
Senior Lecturer in Economic History
University of Strathclyde

in preparation

THE FACTORY SYSTEM   VOLUME II: THE FACTORY SYSTEM AND SOCIETY
J. T. Ward
Senior Lecturer in Economic History
University of Strathclyde

POOR LAW
Michael E. Rose
Lecturer in History, University of Manchester

READINGS IN THE DEVELOPMENT OF ECONOMIC ANALYSIS
R. D. C. Black
Professor of Economics, The Queen's University of Belfast

SOURCES FOR SOCIAL AND ECONOMIC HISTORY

NORMAN McCORD

Reader in Modern History
University of Newcastle upon Tyne

Free Trade

THEORY AND PRACTICE FROM ADAM SMITH TO KEYNES

BARNES & NOBLE, Inc.
NEW YORK
PUBLISHERS & BOOKSELLERS SINCE 1873

First Published in the United States, 1970
by Barnes & Noble, Inc.
ISBN 389-04042-8

Printed in Great Britain

Contents

Introduction

The object of this book is to present a varied selection of documents relating to the development of Britain's Free Trade policy, and its subsequent abandonment. For very many years the question of Free Trade *versus* Protection was the most important topic at issue in the country's economic policy, but the interest of this conflict is not simply in the realm of economic theory. The story of Free Trade in Britain is an object lesson in the interaction of economic, political and social history. Both the implementation of Free Trade and its repudiation depended upon the enactment of legislation; the story cannot be rendered intelligible by a simple anthology from the works of economic theorists. This selection of source material, therefore, includes a good deal from the political arena, ranging from crude propaganda during the agitations of 1838–46 and 1903–6 to speeches in Parliament and other more respectable forms of polemic. In addition, however, extracts are given from the works of such major writers as Adam Smith, Mill and Keynes.

A long key passage from Adam Smith's *The Wealth of Nations* is the first choice. This forms an admirable jumping-off point for any study of Free Trade in Britain. It is true that in recent years it has become almost an occupational disease of historians of economic thought to trace back the ideas expounded in *The Wealth of Nations* to the works of earlier writers. This does not, however, seriously diminish the importance of Adam Smith's work, which must be accounted among the most effective and influential books in the history of economics. Its readily intelli-

gible arguments and lucid exposition provided a clear intellectual justification for the abandonment of mercantilist con-
ceptions and policies. Even if many of its ideas had been fore-
shadowed by earlier writers, there is ample testimony to the
significance of this book in the tributes paid to Adam Smith not
only by subsequent economic theorists but also by a whole
series of prominent politicians whose practical actions owed
something to his arguments.

In the early decades of the nineteenth century the ideas of
Adam Smith and his disciples spread, especially inside influential groups in that very unequal society. Power in early
nineteenth-century Britain was firmly in the hands of a ruling
minority, and by the 1820s and 1830s there was widespread
support within that ruling minority for the relaxation of much
of the old code of regulation of commerce by tariffs. This is not
to say that Free Trade on Cobdenite lines had won the day, but
certainly both Tory and Whig governments proved to be advocates of 'Freer Trade', as the tariff cuts introduced by Huskisson
in the 1820s and Poulett Thomson in the 1830s demonstrated.
All these moves marked steps in the dismantling of the old tariff
system. One very great obstacle to Free Trade still remained,
however, in the shape of the Corn Laws enacted to protect
British agriculture from foreign competition. By the 1840s the
Corn Laws stood out as the major remaining bastion of Protection, while tariffs on other imports had been very substan-
tially diminished. This situation, together with the spread of
Free Trade ideas and the slump of the later 1830s and early
1840s, ushered in the crisis over economic policy in the 1840s,
and paved the way for the eventual triumph of Free Trade.
This crisis, and the activities of the Anti-Corn Law League,
cannot, however, be seen simply as an academic argument
about the economic benefits of agricultural protection, for political and social factors also entered largely into the conflict. The
campaign against the Corn Laws was entered into partly to
provide a rallying-point for radical energies, and a focus which
could bring together all the varied interests that for one reason

or another disliked the social and political predominance of the landed interest in Britain. The symbolic importance of the Corn Laws, both for attackers and defenders, provided much of the heat in the conflict of the 1840s, and the victory of Free Trade here proved a decisive one. When that major bastion of Protection had fallen in 1846 the remaining outworks of the old protective system could be dismantled with relative ease.

It is noticeable, however, that the crucial factor in repealing the Corn Laws was not oratory, or the arguments or the political power of the Anti-Corn Law League, but the marshalling of Conservative and Whig votes behind the proposals of Sir Robert Peel, whose conversion to Free Trade seems to have owed something to the arguments propounded by contemporary political economists, but more perhaps to his pragmatic experience of the results of tariff cuts carried out by himself and his predecessors in office.

The victory of Free Trade in 1846 had lasting results. Those who had contributed to the victory were concerned now to emphasise its enduring importance. Growing prosperity at mid-century seemed to confirm fully the merits of the policy adopted, and by 1852 every major political group supported Free Trade as Britain's natural economic policy. Indeed belief in the economic and moral rightness of Free Trade became a national dogma. British economists were overwhelmingly behind it; those who opposed Free Trade were a small and ineffective minority, and the works of such notable Continental protectionists as List were little regarded. Free Trade seemed impregnable in Britain.

The first attempts to reverse the verdict of 1846 seemed merely to underline its validity. By the 1870s and 1880s some sections of British industry were facing increasing difficulties, partly because of the development of foreign competition. It did not then seem quite so certain that Britain's role as 'the workshop of the world' was permanently secure. There had always been a few eccentrics who denied the doctrine of Free Trade, and now the 'Fair Trade' movement made some stir. The very

name, however, is a testimony to the strength of Free Trade—
Protection was still a word to be avoided whenever possible by
the tariff reformers of the late nineteenth and early twentieth
centuries. For a while in the 1880s some members of the Conservative Party flirted with Fair Trade, with its heresies of reciprocity and retaliation in duties. The flirtation never produced
practical results, however, because of the obvious strength of
Free Trade sentiment, and because the need to co-operate with
the Liberal Unionists, who remained wedded to Free Trade,
inhibited the Conservatives after the Home Rule crisis of
1885–6. Gladstonian Liberalism never wavered in its adherence
to the holy standard of Free Trade. Fair Trade owed its existence to the enthusiastic support of a small number of vested
interests, and never made very great headway.

Early in the new century a more impressive attack on Free
Trade came in Joseph Chamberlain's crusade for Tariff Reform.
Imperialism had played a part in anti-Free Trade moves in the
Fair Trade days of the 1870s and 1880s, but was now more
active and more strident. The conception of an Imperial Zoll-
verein, or common market, was cardinal to Chamberlain's
schemes, though this was not the whole story, for protection of
British industries and the use of tariffs to finance major welfare
benefits for the poor also appeared in his schemes for Tariff
Reform. Economic theorists like Alfred Marshall were now less
concerned in their writings with the old arguments about Free
Trade and Protection, and more involved in increasingly
sophisticated elaborations of marginal utility analysis. However,
among academic economists dominant opinion still regarded
Free Trade as the correct policy for Britain to follow.

Chamberlain's crusade for Tariff Reform split the Unionist
coalition which had dominated British politics since the Home
Rule crisis of 1885–6, and the general election of 1906 brought
overwhelming victory to a Liberal government determined to
maintain the traditional Free Trade posture. Tariff Reform was
beaten for the time being, but it was not dead. Fair Trade and
then Tariff Reform had awoken echoes in the Conservative

Party, and men like Bonar Law and Baldwin—both, significantly enough, strongly linked to the iron industry, an interest worried by foreign competition—carried on Chamberlain's work in the years after 1906.

Baldwin became Prime Minister in 1923, and before the end of the year made his move against Free Trade. In a sudden general election he asked for a free hand to use tariffs if necessary to protect threatened British interests and fight unemployment. The Liberal and Labour parties both fought in defence of the traditional Free Trade policy, and its strength was demonstrated by the Conservative defeat, which led to the formation of the first Labour government and Baldwin's inaction on the tariff issue when he returned to power after that brief interlude.

Once again protectionist ideas had been beaten off, but the devoted support for Free Trade could not survive the battering it received in the economic crisis of 1929–31. Much more effective than the arguments of J. M. Keynes were the armies of unemployed, and there was widespread acceptance that new methods must be tried. The National government, in which Joseph Chamberlain's younger son Neville was Chancellor of the Exchequer, adopted a general tariff in 1932, amidst the lamentations of doctrinaire Free Traders; and with this the long rule of Free Trade over the British economy had ended. The selection of documents offered here ends with an essay by Keynes, written during the crisis of 1931, which forms an appropriate contrast in ideas and arguments to the passage from *The Wealth of Nations* with which the first section begins.

PART ONE

The Rise of Free Trade

Free-trade ideas gained increasing currency in the
decades before the decisive struggle over the Corn
Laws in the 1840s.

The best starting point is Adam Smith's *Wealth
of Nations*. Few books can ever have produced such widespread
and clearly demonstrable effects as this. Its attractive style of
argument and presentation was joined to clear thinking. Smith
argued that division of labour lay at the heart of increased
productivity, and that division of labour depended on the
existence of opportunities for exchange, which should be as
wide as possible. The passage cited here is the fullest presentation of Adam Smith's arguments for freedom of trade (Document 1).

William Pitt the Younger was the first statesman of major
importance to seek to apply Adam Smith's precepts in practice.
One device he employed was a treaty of commerce with France,
in which mutual tariff concessions were to be made. Here (2) we
have an excerpt from a speech in which he argued for these
proposals before the House of Commons in Committee.

Free-trade ideas continued to gain ground in the early decades
of the nineteenth century, though in some important sectors of
the economy protection remained sacrosanct. The Corn Law of
1815 placed high tariffs on agricultural produce, but it was
opposed, even in the highest reaches of contemporary society.
The journals of the House of Lords contain a protest of considerable interest (3) signed by eleven peers, including two royal
dukes.

Naturally enough, perhaps, free-trade ideas spread easily among importers and tradesmen. One protest against the enactment of the 1815 Corn Law which caused some stir was a petition of 1820 signed by a group of London merchants, but drafted for them by a political economist (4).

In political circles similar developments were taking place. In the 1820s and 1830s both Tory and Whig governments moved to reduce tariff barriers. A foreshadowing of the greater struggle ahead came in 1827–8, when the Tory ministers sought to modify the 1815 Corn Law. A new Corn Law was passed with considerable difficulty in 1828, introducing the principle of a sliding scale of duties at a level appreciably below that of 1815. Huskisson was the main architect of this move, and we have here (5) an excerpt from one of his speeches on this issue, ending with a spirited passage condemning the rigidity of the 1815 Corn Law.

Meanwhile, in theoretical expositions of political economy, the ideas of Adam Smith, and their subsequent development by other writers, continued to hold a commanding influence. This first section ends with a short passage from McCulloch (6), which well illustrates this situation. The book was first published in 1837, when we may consider that the scene was set for the decisive struggle over the Corn Laws which was to mark the next decade.

1 Adam Smith   The Wealth of Nations

Adam Smith (1723–90) is considered to be the founder of the modern subject of economics. He was educated at Glasgow University, and then at Balliol College, Oxford. He made his name first as a moral philosopher, holding in succession the chairs of logic and of moral philosophy at Glasgow, and publishing his *Theory of the Moral Sentiments* in 1759. He then accepted an offer to become tutor to the young Duke of Buccleuch, which enabled him to travel abroad with his pupil, and from the mid-1760s to live upon a comfortable pension from the Duke. He moved in distinguished intellectual circles, associating with Hume and Dr Johnson at home, Voltaire and

Turgot abroad. His travels and foreign contacts were in part responsible for his interest in economic questions, which culminated in 1776 in the publication of *The Wealth of Nations*, a book which influenced not only future generations of economic theorists, but also important political figures of his own day, notably the younger Pitt.

Of Restraints upon the Importation from Foreign Countries of such Goods as can be Produced at Home

By restraining, either by high duties, or by absolute prohibitions, the importation of such goods from foreign countries as can be produced at home, the monopoly of the home market is more or less secured to the domestic industry employed in producing them. Thus the prohibition of importing either live cattle or salt provisions from foreign countries secures to the graziers of Great Britain the monopoly of the home market for butcher's meat. The high duties upon the importation of corn, which in times of moderate plenty amount to a prohibition, give a like advantage to the growers of that commodity. The prohibition of the importation of foreign woollens is equally favourable to the woollen manufacturers. The silk manufacture, though altogether employed upon foreign materials, has lately obtained the same advantage. The linen manufacture has not yet obtained it, but is making great strides towards it. Many other sorts of manufacturers have, in the same manner, obtained in Great Britain, either altogether, or very nearly a monopoly against their countrymen. The variety of goods of which the importation into Great Britain is prohibited, either absolutely, or under certain circumstances, greatly exceeds what can easily be suspected by those who are not well acquainted with the laws of the customs.

That this monopoly of the home-market frequently gives great encouragement to that particular species of industry which enjoys it, and frequently turns towards that employment a greater share of both the labour and stock of the society than would otherwise have gone to it, cannot be doubted. But whether

B

it tends either to increase the general industry of the society, or to give it the most advantageous direction, is not, perhaps, altogether so evident.

The general industry of the society never can exceed what the capital of the society can employ. As the number of workmen that can be kept in employment by any particular person must bear a certain proportion to his capital, so the number of those that can be continually employed by all the members of a great society, must bear a certain proportion to the whole capital of that society, and never can exceed that proportion. No regulation of commerce can increase the quantity of industry in any society beyond what its capital can maintain. It can only divert a part of it into a direction into which it might not otherwise have gone; and it is by no means certain that this artificial direction is likely to be more advantageous to the society than that into which it would have gone of its own accord.

Every individual is continually exerting himself to find out the most advantageous employment for whatever capital he can command. It is his own advantage, indeed, and not that of the society which he has in view. But the study of his own advantage naturally, or rather necessarily leads him to prefer that employment which is most advantageous to the society.

First, every individual endeavours to employ his capital as near home as he can, and consequently as much as he can in the support of domestic industry; provided always that he can thereby obtain the ordinary, or not a great deal less than the ordinary profits of stock.

Thus, upon equal or nearly equal profits, every wholesale merchant naturally prefers the home-trade to the foreign trade of consumption, and the foreign trade of consumption to the carrying trade. In the home-trade his capital is never so long out of his sight as it frequently is in the foreign trade of consumption. He can know better the character and situation of the persons whom he trusts, and if he should happen to be deceived, he knows better the laws of the country from which he must seek redress. In the carrying trade, the capital of the merchant is, as it were, divided between two foreign countries, and no part of it is ever necessarily brought home, or placed under his own immediate view and command. The capital which an Amsterdam merchant employs in carrying corn from Konnigsberg to Lisbon, and fruit and wine from Lisbon to Konnigsberg, must generally be the one-half of it at Konnigsberg and the other half at Lisbon. No part of it need ever come to Amsterdam. The natural residence of such a merchant should either be at Konnigsberg or Lisbon, and it can only be some very particular circumstances which can make him prefer the residence of Amsterdam. The uneasiness, however, which he feels at being separated so far from his capital, generally determines him to bring part both of the Konnigsberg goods which he destines for the market of Lisbon, and of the Lisbon goods which he destines for that of Konnigsberg, to Amsterdam: and though this necessarily subjects him to a double charge of loading and unloading, as well as to the payment of some duties and customs, yet for the sake of having some part of his capital always under his own view and command, he willingly submits to this extraordinary charge; and it is in this manner that every country which has any considerable share of the carrying trade, becomes always the emporium, or general market, for the goods of all the different countries whose trade it carries on. The merchant, in order to save a second loading and unloading, endeavours always to sell in the home-market as much of the goods of all those different countries as he can, and thus, so far as he can, to convert his carrying trade into a foreign trade of consumption. A merchant, in the same manner, who is engaged in the foreign trade of consumption, when he collects goods for foreign markets, will always be glad, upon equal or nearly equal profits, to sell as great a part of them at home as he can. He saves himself the risk and trouble of exportation, when, so far as he can, he thus converts his foreign trade of consumption into a home-trade. Home is in this manner the center, if I may say so, round which the capitals of the inhabitants of every country are continually circulating, and towards which they are always tending, though by particular causes they may sometimes

be driven off and repelled from it towards more distant employments. But a capital employed in the home-trade, it has already
been shown, necessarily puts into motion a greater quantity of
domestic industry, and gives revenue and employment to a
greater number of the inhabitants of the country, than an equal
capital employed in the foreign trade of consumption: and one
employed in the foreign trade of consumption has the same
advantage over an equal capital employed in the carrying trade.
Upon equal, or only nearly equal profits, therefore, every individual naturally inclines to employ his capital in the manner in
which it is likely to afford the greatest support to domestic
industry, and to give revenue and employment to the greatest
number of people of his own country.

Secondly, every individual who employs his capital in the
support of domestic industry, necessarily endeavours so to direct
that industry, that its produce may be of the greatest possible
value.

The produce of industry is what it adds to the subject or
materials upon which it is employed. In proportion as the value
of this produce is great or small, so will likewise be the profits of
the employer. But it is only for the sake of profit that any man
employs a capital in the support of industry; and he will always,
therefore, endeavour to employ it in the support of that industry
of which the produce is likely to be of the greatest value, or to
exchange for the greatest quantity either of money or of other
goods.

But the annual revenue of every society is always precisely
equal to the exchangeable value of the whole annual produce of
its industry, or rather is precisely the same thing with that
exchangeable value. As every individual, therefore, endeavours
as much as he can both to employ his capital in the support of
domestic industry, and so to direct that industry that its produce
may be of the greatest value; every individual necessarily labours
to render the annual revenue of the society as great as he can.
He generally, indeed, neither intends to promote the public
interest, nor knows how much he is promoting it. By preferring

the support of domestic to that of foreign industry, he intends only his own security; and by directing that industry in such a manner as its produce may be of the greatest value, he intends only his own gain, and he is in this, as in many other cases, led by an invisible hand to promote an end which was no part of his intention. Nor is it always the worse for the society that it was no part of it. By pursuing his own interest he frequently promotes that of the society more effectually than when he really intends to promote it. I have never known much good done by those who affected to trade for the public good. It is an affectation, indeed, not very common among merchants, and very few words need be employed in dissuading them from it.

What is the species of domestic industry which his capital can employ, and of which the produce is likely to be of the greatest value, every individual, it is evident, can, in his local situation, judge much better than any statesman or lawgiver can do for him. The statesman, who should attempt to direct private people in what manner they ought to employ their capitals, would not only load himself with a most unnecessary attention, but assume an authority which could safely be trusted, not only to no single person, but to no council or senate whatever, and which would no-where be so dangerous as in the hands of a man who had folly and presumption enough to fancy himself fit to exercise it.

To give the monopoly of the home-market to the produce of domestic industry, in any particular art or manufacture, is in some measure to direct private people in what manner they ought to employ their capitals, and must, in almost all cases, be either a useless or a hurtful regulation. If the produce of domestic can be brought there as cheap as that of foreign industry, the regulation is evidently useless. If it cannot, it must generally be hurtful. It is the maxim of every prudent master of a family, never to attempt to make at home what it will cost him more to make than to buy. The taylor does not attempt to make his own shoes, but buys them of the shoemaker. The shoemaker does not attempt to make his own clothes, but employs a taylor. The farmer attempts to make neither the one nor the other, but employs those different artificers. All of them find it for their interest to employ their whole industry in a way in which they have some advantage over their neighbours, and to purchase with a part of its produce, or what is the same thing, with the price of a part of it, whatever else they have occasion for.

What is prudence in the conduct of every private family, can scarce be folly in that of a great kingdom. If a foreign country can supply us with a commodity cheaper than we ourselves can make it, better buy it of them with some part of the produce of our own industry, employed in a way in which we have some advantage. The general industry of the country, being always in proportion to the capital which employs it, will not thereby be diminished, no more than that of the above-mentioned artificers; but only left to find out the way in which it can be employed with the greatest advantage. It is certainly not employed to the greatest advantage, when it is thus directed towards an object which it can buy cheaper than it can make. The value of its annual produce is certainly more or less diminished, when it is thus turned away from producing commodities evidently of more value than the commodity which it is directed to produce. According to the supposition, that commodity could be purchased from foreign countries cheaper than it can be made at home. It could, therefore, have been purchased with a part only of the commodities, or, what is the same thing, with a part only of the price of the commodities, which the industry employed by an equal capital would have produced at home, had it been left to follow its natural course. The industry of the country, therefore, is thus turned away from a more, to a less advantageous employment, and the exchangeable value of its annual produce, instead of being increased, according to the intention of the lawgiver, must necessarily be diminished by every such regulation.

By means of such regulations, indeed, a particular manufacture may sometimes be acquired sooner than it could have been otherwise, and after a certain time may be made at home as cheap or cheaper than in the foreign country. But though the industry of the society may be thus carried with advantage into a particular channel sooner than it could have been otherwise, it will by no means follow that the sum total, either of its industry, or of its revenue, can ever be augmented by any such regulation. The industry of the society can augment only in proportion as its capital augments, and its capital can augment only in proportion to what can be gradually saved out of its revenue. But the immediate effect of every such regulation is to diminish its revenue, and what diminishes its revenue is certainly not very likely to augment its capital faster than it would have augmented of its own accord, had both capital and industry been left to find out their natural employments.

Though for want of such regulations the society should never acquire the proposed manufacture, it would not, upon that account, necessarily be the poorer in any one period of its duration. In every period of its duration its whole capital and industry might still have been employed, though upon different objects, in the manner that was most advantageous at the time. In every period its revenue might have been the greatest which its capital could afford, and both capital and revenue might have been augmented with the greatest possible rapidity.

The natural advantages which one country has over another in producing particular commodities are sometimes so great, that it is acknowledged by all the world to be in vain to struggle with them. By means of glasses, hotbeds, and hotwalls, very good grapes can be raised in Scotland, and very good wine too can be made of them at about thirty times the expence for which at least equally good can be brought from foreign countries. Would it be a reasonable law to prohibit the importation of all foreign wines, merely to encourage the making of claret and burgundy in Scotland? But if there would be a manifest absurdity in turning towards any employment, thirty times more of the capital and industry of the country, than would be necessary to purchase from foreign countries an equal quantity of the commodities wanted, there must be an absurdity, though not altogether so glaring, yet exactly of the same kind, in turning towards any such employment a thirtieth, or even a three hundredth part more of either. Whether the advantages which one country has over another, be natural or acquired, is in this respect of no consequence. As long as the one country has those advantages, and the other wants them, it will always be more advantageous for the latter, rather to buy of the former than to make. It is an acquired advantage only, which one artificer has over his neighbour, who exercises another trade; and yet they both find it more advantageous to buy of one another, than to make what does not belong to their particular trades.

Merchants and manufacturers are the people who derive the greatest advantage from this monopoly of the home-market. The prohibition of the importation of foreign cattle, and of salt provisions, together with the high duties upon foreign corn, which in times of moderate plenty amount to a prohibition, are not near so advantageous to the graziers and farmers of Great Britain, as other regulations of the same kind are to its merchants and manufacturers. Manufactures, those of the finer kind especially, are more easily transported from one country to another than corn or cattle. It is in the fetching and carrying manufactures, accordingly, that foreign trade is chiefly employed. In manufactures, a very small advantage will enable foreigners to undersell our own workmen, even in the home market. It will require a very great one to enable them to do so in the rude produce of the soil. If the free importation of foreign manufactures were permitted, several of the home manufactures would probably suffer, and some of them, perhaps, go to ruin altogether, and a considerable part of the stock and industry at present employed in them, would be forced to find out some other employment. But the freest importation of the rude produce of the soil could have no such effect upon the agriculture of the country.

If the importation of foreign cattle, for example, were made ever so free, so few could be imported, that the grazing trade of Great Britain could be little affected by it. Live cattle are, perhaps, the only commodity of which the transportation is more expensive by sea than by land. By land they carry themselves to market. By sea, not only the cattle, but their food and their water too, must be carried at no small expence and inconveniency. The short sea between Ireland and Great Britain, indeed, renders the importation of Irish cattle more easy. But though the free importation of them, which was lately permitted only for a limited time, were rendered perpetual, it could have no considerable effect upon the interest of the graziers of Great Britain. Those parts of Great Britain which border upon the Irish sea are all grazing countries. Irish cattle could never be imported for their use, but must be drove through those very extensive countries, at no small expence and inconveniency, before they could arrive at their proper market. Fat cattle could not be drove so far. Lean cattle, therefore, only could be imported, and such importation could interfere, not with the interest of the feeding or fattening countries, to which, by reducing the price of lean cattle, it would rather be advantageous, but with that of the breeding countries only. The small number of Irish cattle imported since their importation was permitted, together with the good price at which lean cattle still continue to sell, seem to demonstrate that even the breeding countries of Great Britain are never likely to be much affected by the free importation of Irish cattle. The common people of Ireland, indeed, are said to have sometimes opposed with violence the exportation of their cattle. But if the exporters had found any great advantage in continuing the trade, they could easily, when the law was on their side, have conquered this mobbish opposition.

Feeding and fattening countries, besides, must always be highly improved, whereas breeding countries are generally uncultivated. The high price of lean cattle, by augmenting the value of uncultivated land, is like a bounty against improvement. To any country which was highly improved throughout, it would be more advantageous to import its lean cattle than to breed them. The province of Holland, accordingly, is said to follow this maxim at present. The mountains of Scotland, Wales and Northumberland, indeed, are countries not capable of much improvement, and seem destined by nature to be the breeding countries of Great Britain. The freest importation of foreign cattle could have no other effect than to hinder those breeding countries from taking advantage of the increasing population and improvement of the rest of the kingdom, from raising their price to an exorbitant height, and from laying a real tax upon all the more improved and cultivated parts of the country.

The freest importation of salt provisions, in the same manner, could have as little effect upon the interest of the graziers of Great Britain as that of live cattle. Salt provisions are not only a very bulky commodity, but when compared with fresh meat, they are a commodity both of worse quality, and as they cost more labour and expence, of higher price. They could never, therefore, come into competition with the fresh meat, though they might with the salt provisions of the country. They might be used for victualling ships for distant voyages, and such like uses, but could never make any considerable part of the food of the people. The small quantity of salt provisions imported from Ireland since their importation was rendered free, is an experimental proof that our graziers have nothing to apprehend from it. It does not appear that the price of butcher's-meat has ever been sensibly affected by it.

Even the free importation of foreign corn could very little affect the interest of the farmers of Great Britain. Corn is a much more bulky commodity than butcher's-meat. A pound of wheat at a penny is as dear as a pound of butcher's-meat at fourpence. The small quantity of foreign corn imported even in times of the greatest scarcity, may satisfy our farmers that they can have nothing to fear from the freest importation. The average quantity imported one year with another, amounts only, according to the very well informed author of the tracts upon the corn trade, to twenty-three thousand seven hundred and twenty-eight quarters of all sorts of grain, and does not exceed the five hundredth and seventy-one part of the annual consumption. But as the bounty upon corn occasions a greater exportation in years of plenty, so it must of consequence occasion a greater importation in years of scarcity, than in the actual state of tillage would otherwise take place. By means of it, the plenty of one year does not compensate the scarcity of another, and as the average quantity exported is necessarily augmented by it, so must likewise, in the actual state of tillage, the average quantity imported. If there were no bounty, as less corn would be exported, so it is probable that, one year with another, less would be imported than at present. The corn merchants, the fetchers and carriers of corn between Great Britain and foreign countries, would have much less employment, and might suffer considerably; but the country gentlemen and farmers could suffer very little. It is in the corn merchants accordingly, rather than in the country gentlemen and farmers, that I have observed the greatest anxiety for the renewal and continuation of the bounty.

Country gentlemen and farmers are, to their great honour, of all people, the least subject to the wretched spirit of monopoly. The undertaker of a great manufactory is sometimes alarmed if another work of the same kind is established within twenty miles of him. The Dutch undertaker of the woollen manufacture at Abbeville stipulated, that no work of the same kind should be established within thirty leagues of that city. Farmers and country gentlemen, on the contrary, are generally disposed rather to promote than to obstruct the cultivation and improvement of their neighbours' farms and estates. They have no secrets, such as those of the greater part of manufacturers, but are generally rather fond of communicating to their neighbours, and of extending as far as possible any new practice which they have found to be advantageous. *Pius Questus*, says old Cato, *stabilissimusque, minimeque invidiosus; minimeque male cogitantes sunt, qui in eo studio occupati sunt*. Country gentlemen and farmers, dispersed in different parts of the country, cannot so easily combine as merchants and manufacturers, who being collected into towns, and accustomed to that exclusive corporation spirit which prevails in them, naturally endeavour to obtain against all their countrymen, the same exclusive privilege which they generally possess against the inhabitants of their respective towns. They accordingly seem to have been the original inventors of those restraints upon the importation of foreign goods, which secure to them the monopoly of the home-market. It was probably in imitation of them, and to put themselves upon a level with those who, they found, were disposed to oppress them, that the country gentlemen and far-mers of Great Britain so far forgot the generosity which is natural to their station, as to demand the exclusive privilege of supplying their countrymen with corn and butcher's-meat. They did not perhaps take time to consider, how much less their interest could be affected by the freedom of trade, than that of the people whose example they followed.

To prohibit by a perpetual law the importation of foreign corn and cattle, is in reality to enact, that the population and industry of the country shall at no time exceed what the rude produce of its own soil can maintain.

There seem, however, to be two cases in which it will generally be advantageous to lay some burden upon foreign, for the en-couragement of domestic industry.

The first is, when some particular sort of industry is necessary for the defence of the country. The defence of Great Britain, for example, depends very much upon the number of its sailors and shipping. The act of navigation, therefore, very properly en-deavours to give the sailors and shipping of Great Britain the monopoly of the trade of their own country, in some cases, by absolute prohibitions, and in others by heavy burdens upon the shipping of foreign countries. The following are the principal dispositions of this act.

First, all ships, of which the owners, masters, and three-fourths of the mariners are not British subjects, are prohibited, upon pain of forfeiting ship and cargo, from trading to the British settle-ments and plantations, or from being employed in the coasting trade of Great Britain.

Secondly, a great variety of the most bulky articles of importa-tion can be brought into Great Britain only, either in such ships as are above described, or in ships of the country where those goods are produced, and of which the owners, masters, and three-fourths of the mariners, are of that particular country; and when imported even in ships of this latter kind, they are subject to double aliens duty. If imported in ships of any other country, the penalty is forfeiture of ship and goods. When this act was made, the Dutch were, what they still are, the great carriers of Europe, and by this regulation they were entirely excluded from being the carriers to Great Britain, or from importing to us the goods of any other European country.

Thirdly, a great variety of the most bulky articles of importation are prohibited from being imported, even in British ships, from any country but that in which they are produced; under pain of forfeiting ship and cargo. This regulation too was probably intended against the Dutch. Holland was then, as now, the great emporium for all European goods, and by this regulation, British ships were hindered from loading in Holland the goods of any other European country.

Fourthly, salt fish of all kinds, whale-fins, whale-bone, oil, and blubber, not caught by and cured on board British vessels, when imported into Great Britain, are subjected to double aliens duty. The Dutch, as they are still the principal, were then the only fishers in Europe that attempted to supply foreign nations with fish. By this regulation, a very heavy burden was laid upon their supplying Great Britain.

When the act of navigation was made, though England and Holland were not actually at war, the most violent animosity subsisted between the two nations. It had begun during the government of the long parliament, which first framed this act, and it broke out soon after in the Dutch wars during that of the Protector and of Charles the Second. It is not impossible, therefore, that some of the regulations of this famous act may have proceeded from national animosity. They are as wise, however, as if they had all been dictated by the most deliberate wisdom. National animosity at that particular time aimed at the very same object which the most deliberate wisdom would have recommended, the diminution of the naval power of Holland, the only naval power which could endanger the security of England.

The act of navigation is not favourable to foreign commerce, or to the growth of that opulence which can arise from it. The interest of a nation in its commercial relations to foreign nations is, like that of a merchant with regard to the different people with whom he deals, to buy as cheap and to sell as dear as possible. But it will be most likely to buy cheap, when by the most perfect freedom of trade it encourages all nations to bring to it the goods which it has occasion to purchase; and, for the same reason, it will be most likely to sell dear, when its markets are thus filled with the greatest number of buyers. The act of navigation, it is true, lays no burden upon foreign ships that come to export the produce of British industry. Even the ancient aliens duty, which used to be paid upon all goods exported as well as imported, has, by several subsequent acts, been taken off from the greater part of the articles of exportation. But if foreigners, either by prohibitions or high duties, are hindered from coming to sell, they cannot always afford to come to buy; because coming without a cargo, they must lose the freight from their own country to Great Britain. By diminishing the number of sellers, therefore, we necessarily diminish that of buyers, and are thus likely not only to buy foreign goods dearer, but to sell our own cheaper, than if there was a more perfect freedom of trade. As defence, however, is of much more importance than opulence, the act of navigation is, perhaps, the wisest of all the commercial regulations of England.

The second case, in which it will generally be advantageous to lay some burden upon foreign for the encouragement of domestic industry, is, when some tax is imposed at home upon the produce of the latter. In this case, it seems reasonable that an equal tax should be imposed upon the like produce of the former. This would not give the monopoly of the home market to domestic industry, nor turn towards a particular employment a greater share of the stock and labour of the country, than what would naturally go to it. It would only hinder any part of what would naturally go to it from being turned away by the tax, into a less natural direction, and would leave the competition between foreign and domestic industry, after the tax, as nearly as possible upon the same footing as before it. In Great Britain, when any such tax is laid upon the produce of domestic industry, it is usual at the same time, in order to stop the clamorous complaints of our merchants and manufacturers, that they will be undersold at home, to lay a much heavier duty upon the importation of all foreign goods of the same kind.

This second limitation of the freedom of trade according to some people should, upon some occasions, be extended much farther than to the precise foreign commodities which could come into competition with those which had been taxed at home. When the necessaries of life have been taxed in any country, it becomes proper, they pretend, to tax not only the like necessaries of life imported from other countries, but all sorts of foreign goods which can come into competition with any thing that is the produce of domestic industry. Subsistence, they say, becomes necessarily dearer in consequence of such taxes; and the price of labour must always rise with the price of the labourers sub- sistence. Every commodity, therefore, which is the produce of domestic industry, though not immediately taxed itself, becomes dearer in consequence of such taxes, because the labour which produces it becomes so. Such taxes, therefore, are really equiva- lent, they say, to a tax upon every particular commodity pro- duced at home. In order to put domestic upon the same footing with foreign industry, therefore, it becomes necessary, they think, to lay some duty upon every foreign commodity, equal to this enhancement of the price of the home commodities with which it can come into competition.

Whether taxes upon the necessaries of life, such as those in Great Britain upon soap, salt, leather, candles, &c. necessarily raise the price of labour, and consequently that of all other commodities, I shall consider hereafter, when I come to treat of taxes. Supposing, however, in the mean time, that they have this effect, and they have it undoubtedly, this general enhancement of the price of all commodities, in consequence of that of labour, is a case which differs in the two following respects from that of a particular commodity, of which the price was enhanced by a particular tax immediately imposed upon it.

First, it might always be known with great exactness how far the price of such a commodity could be enhanced by such a tax: but how far the general enhancement of the price of labour might affect that of every different commodity about which labour was employed, could never be known with any tolerable exactness. It would be impossible, therefore, to proportion with any tolerable exactness the tax upon every foreign, to this enhancement of the price of every home commodity.

Secondly, taxes upon the necessaries of life have nearly the same effect upon the circumstances of the people as a poor soil and a bad climate. Provisions are thereby rendered dearer in the same manner as if it required extraordinary labour and expence to raise them. As in the natural scarcity arising from soil and climate, it would be absurd to direct the people in what manner they ought to employ their capitals and industry, so is it likewise in the artificial scarcity arising from such taxes. To be left to accommodate, as well as they could, their industry to their situation, and to find out those employments in which, notwithstanding their unfavourable circumstances, they might have some advantage either in the home or in the foreign market, is what in both cases would evidently be most for their advantage. To lay a new tax upon them, because they are already overburdened with taxes, and because they already pay too dear for the necessaries of life, to make them likewise pay too dear for the greater part of other commodities, is certainly a most absurd way of making amends.

Such taxes, when they have grown up to a certain height, are a curse equal to the barrenness of the earth and the inclemency of the heavens; and yet it is in the richest and most industrious countries that they have been most generally imposed. No other countries could support so great a disorder. As the strongest bodies only can live and enjoy health, under an unwholesome regimen; so the nations only, that in every sort of industry have the greatest natural and acquired advantages, can subsist and prosper under such taxes. Holland is the country in Europe in which they abound most, and which from peculiar circumstances continues to prosper, not by means of them, as has been most absurdly supposed, but in spite of them.

As there are two cases in which it will generally be advantageous to lay some burden upon foreign, for the encouragement of domestic industry; so there are two others in which it may sometimes be a matter of deliberation; in the one, how far it is proper to continue the free importation of certain foreign goods; and in the other, how far, or in what manner, it may be proper to restore that free importation after it has been for some time interrupted.

The case in which it may sometimes be a matter of deliberation how far it is proper to continue the free importation of certain foreign goods, is, when some foreign nation restrains by high duties or prohibitions the importation of some of our manufactures into their country. Revenge in this case naturally dictates retaliation, and that we should impose the like duties and prohibitions upon the importation of some or all of their manufactures into ours. Nations accordingly seldom fail to retaliate in this manner. The French have been particularly forward to favour their own manufactures by restraining the importation of such foreign goods as could come into competition with them. In this consisted a great part of the policy of Mr Colbert, who, notwithstanding his great abilities, seems in this case to have been imposed upon by the sophistry of merchants and manufacturers, who are always demanding a monopoly against their countrymen. It is at present the opinion of the most intelligent men in France that his operations of this kind have not been beneficial to his country. That minister, by the tarif of 1667, imposed very high duties upon a great number of foreign manufactures. Upon his refusing to moderate them in favour of the Dutch, they in 1671 prohibited the importation of the wines, brandies and manufactures of France. The war of 1672 seems to have been in part occasioned by this commercial dispute. The peace of Nimeguen put an end to it in 1678, by moderating some of those duties in

C

favour of the Dutch, who in consequence took off their prohibition. It was about the same time that the French and English began mutually to oppress each other's industry, by the like duties and prohibitions, of which the French, however, seem to have set the first example. The spirit of hostility, which has subsisted between the two nations ever since, has hitherto hindered them from being moderated on either side. In 1697 the English prohibited the importation of bonelace, the manufacture of Flanders. The government of that country, at that time under the dominion of Spain, prohibited in return the importation of English woollens. In 1700, the prohibition of importing bonelace into England, was taken off upon condition that the importation of English woollens into Flanders should be put on the same footing as before.

There may be good policy in retaliations of this kind, when there is a probability that they will procure the repeal of the high duties or prohibitions complained of. The recovery of a great foreign market will generally more than compensate the transitory inconveniency of paying dearer during a short time for some sorts of goods. To judge whether such retaliations are likely to produce such an effect, does not, perhaps, belong so much to the science of a legislator, whose deliberations ought to be governed by general principles which are always the same, as to the skill of that insidious and crafty animal, vulgarly called a statesman or politician, whose councils are directed by the momentary fluctuations of affairs. When there is no probability that any such repeal can be procured, it seems a bad method of compensating the injury done to certain classes of our people, to do another injury ourselves, not only to those classes, but to almost all other classes of them. When our neighbours prohibit some manufacture of ours, we generally prohibit, not only the same, for that alone would seldom affect them considerably, but some other manufacture of theirs. This may no doubt give encouragement to some particular class of workmen among ourselves, and by excluding some of their rivals, may enable them to raise their price in the home-market. Those workmen, however, who suf-

fered by our neighbours prohibition will not be benefited by
ours. On the contrary, they and almost all the other classes of
our citizens will thereby be obliged to pay dearer than before for
certain goods. Every such law, therefore, imposes a real tax upon
the whole country, not in favour of that particular class of workmen who were injured by our neighbours prohibition, but of
some other class.

The case in which it may sometimes be a matter of deliberation, how far, or in what manner, it is proper to restore the free
importation of foreign goods, after it has been for some time
interrupted, is, when particular manufactures, by means of high
duties or prohibitions upon all foreign goods which can come
into competition with them, have been so far extended as to
employ a great multitude of hands. Humanity may in this case
require that the freedom of trade should be restored only by slow
gradations, and with a good deal of reserve and circumspection.
Were those high duties and prohibitions taken away all at once,
cheaper foreign goods of the same kind might be poured so fast
into the home market, as to deprive all at once many thousands
of our people of their ordinary employment and means of subsistence. The disorder which this would occasion might no doubt
be very considerable. It would in all probability, however, be
much less than is commonly imagined, for the two following
reasons:

First, all those manufactures, of which any part is commonly
exported to other European countries without a bounty, could
be very little affected by the freest importation of foreign goods.
Such manufactures must be sold as cheap abroad as any other
foreign goods of the same quality and kind, and consequently
must be sold cheaper at home. They would still, therefore, keep
possession of the home market, and though a capricious man of
fashion might sometimes prefer foreign wares, merely because
they were foreign, to cheaper and better goods of the same kind
that were made at home, this folly could, from the nature of
things, extend to so few, that it could make no sensible impression
upon the general employment of the people. But a great part of

all the different branches of our woollen manufacture, of our tanned leather, and of our hardware, are annually exported to other European countries without any bounty, and these are the manufactures which employ the greatest number of hands. The silk, perhaps, is the manufacture which would suffer the most by this freedom of trade, and after it the linen, though the latter much less than the former.

Secondly, though a great number of people should, by thus restoring the freedom of trade, be thrown all at once out of their ordinary employment and common method of subsistence, it would by no means follow that they would thereby be deprived either of employment or subsistence. By the reduction of the army and navy at the end of the late war, more than a hundred thousand soldiers and seamen, a number equal to what is employed in the greatest manufactures, were all at once thrown out of their ordinary employment; but, though they no doubt suffered some inconveniency, they were not thereby deprived of all employment and subsistence. The greater part of the seamen, it is probable, gradually betook themselves to the merchant-service as they could find occasion, and in the meantime both they and the soldiers were absorbed in the great mass of the people, and employed in a great variety of occupations. Not only no great convulsion, but no sensible disorder arose from so great a change in the situation of more than a hundred thousand men, all accustomed to the use of arms, and many of them to rapine and plunder. The number of vagrants was scarce any-where sensibly increased by it, even the wages of labour were not reduced by it in any occupation, so far as I have been able to learn, except in that of seamen in the merchant-service. But if we compare together the habits of a soldier and of any sort of manufacturer, we shall find that those of the latter do not tend so much to disqualify him from being employed in a new trade, as those of the former from being employed in any. The manufacturer has always been accustomed to look for his subsistence from his labour only: the soldier to expect it from his pay. Application and industry have been familiar to the one; idleness and dissipation to the other. But it is surely much easier to change the direction of industry from one sort of labour to another, than to turn idleness and dissipation to any. To the greater part of manufactures besides, it has already been observed, there are other collateral manufactures of so similar a nature, that a workman can easily transfer his industry from one of them to another. The greater part of such workmen too are occasionally employed in country labour. The stock which employed them in a particular manufacture before, will still remain in the country to employ an equal number of people in some other way. The capital of the country remaining the same, the demand for labour will likewise be the same, or very nearly the same, though it may be exerted in different places and for different occupations. Soldiers and seamen, indeed, when discharged from the king's service, are at liberty to exercise any trade, within any town or place of Great Britain or Ireland. Let the same natural liberty of exercising what species of industry they please, be restored to all his majesty's subjects, in the same manner as to soldiers and seamen; that is, break down the exclusive privileges of corporations, and repeal the statute of apprenticeship, both which are real encroachments upon natural liberty, and add to these the repeal of the law of settlements, so that a poor workman, when thrown out of employment either in one trade or in one place, may seek for it in another trade or in another place, without the fear either of a prosecution or of a removal, and neither the public nor the individuals will suffer much more from the occasional disbanding some particular classes of manufacturers, than from that of soldiers. Our manufacturers have no doubt great merit with their country, but they cannot have more than those who defend it with their blood, nor deserve to be treated with more delicacy.

To expect, indeed, that the freedom of trade should ever be entirely restored in Great Britain, is as absurd as to expect that an Oceana or Utopia should ever be established in it. Not only the prejudices of the public, but what is much more unconquerable, the private interests of many individuals, irresistibly oppose it. Were the officers of the army to oppose with the same zeal and unanimity any reduction in the number of forces, with which master manufacturers set themselves against every law that is likely to increase the number of their rivals in the home market; were the former to animate their soldiers, in the same manner as the latter enflame their workmen, to attack with violence and outrage the proposers of any such regulation; to attempt to reduce the army would be as dangerous as it has now become to attempt to diminish in any respect the monopoly which our manufacturers have obtained against us. This monopoly has so much increased the number of some particular tribes of them, that, like an overgrown standing army, they have become formidable to the government, and upon many occasions intimidate the legislature. The member of parliament who supports every proposal for strengthening this monopoly, is sure to acquire not only the reputation of understanding trade, but great popularity and influence with an order of men whose numbers and wealth render them of great importance. If he opposes them, on the contrary, and still more if he has authority enough to be able to thwart them, neither the most acknowledged probity, nor the highest rank, nor the greatest public services, can protect him from the most infamous abuse and detraction, from personal insults, nor sometimes from real danger, arising from the insolent outrage of furious and disappointed monopolists.

The undertaker of a great manufacture, who, by the home markets being suddenly laid open to the competition of foreigners, should be obliged to abandon his trade, would no doubt suffer very considerably. That part of his capital which had usually been employed in purchasing materials and in paying his workmen, might, without much difficulty, perhaps, find another employment. But that part of it which was fixed in workhouses, and in the instruments of trade, could scarce be disposed of without considerable loss. The equitable regard, therefore, to his interest requires that changes of this kind should never be introduced suddenly, but slowly, gradually, and after a very long warning. The legislature, were it possible that its deliberations could be always directed, not by the clamorous importunity of partial interests, but by an extensive view of the general good, ought upon this very account, perhaps, to be particularly careful neither to establish any new monopolies of this kind, nor to extend further those which are already established. Every such regulation introduces some degree of real disorder into the constitution of the state, which it will be difficult afterwards to cure without occasioning another disorder.

How far it may be proper to impose taxes upon the importation of foreign goods, in order, not to prevent their importation, but to raise a revenue for government, I shall consider hereafter when I come to treat of taxes. Taxes imposed with a view to prevent, or even diminish importation, are evidently as destructive of the revenue of the customs as of the freedom of trade. E. Cannan (ed). *The Wealth of Nations*, Vol I, pp 418–36, London, 1961

---

2 William Pitt the Younger   Speech in Parliament

William Pitt the Younger (1759–1806) was the second son of the Elder Pitt. He was Prime Minister from 1783 till 1801, and again in 1804–6. In his first years as premier, one of his most important objectives was to effect an economic recovery from the ill-effects of defeat in the War of American Independence. He improved financial administration, took steps against smuggling, and improved government organisation in a variety of ways. In his attempts to stimulate British commerce he introduced proposals for new commercial arrangements with Ireland and with France, both of which aimed at greater freedom of trade. His Irish proposals were defeated by a factious alliance between British vested interests and the Whig opposition. Fox and his allies also sought to defeat the proposals for a commercial treaty with France, but here Pitt had his way, though the outbreak of the French Revolution three years later, and subsequently war between Britain and France, nullified the treaty of 1786. The aim of the agreement had been to facilitate trade between the two countries by reciprocal tariff reductions. In this passage Pitt is defending his proposals for the treaty with France before the House of Commons in Committee.

———

Great and various were the objects of this treaty; but the resolutions which he should have the honour to propose that evening, would lie in a narrow compass, and be easily embraced. It was not his intention to draw the committee to any general resolution which should involve the measures necessary to be taken in future, nor need gentlemen be alarmed by the groundless idea of being committed by one question to all the important details necessary to the full establishment of the system. Several observations had been made respecting the navigation laws and maritime regulations, upon which, as they did not come within the scope of his motion to the committee, and more properly belonged to the prerogative and the executive government, he would forbear offering any remarks. He meant only to submit to them certain leading resolutions, tending merely to the commercial establishment, and they were founded on the 6th and 11th articles of the Treaty. The result of the Resolutions was precisely this:

1. That the committee should agree, that all articles not enumerated and specified in the tariff should be importable into this country, on terms as favourable as those of the most countenanced nation, excepting always the power of preferring Portugal, under the provisions of the Methuen Treaty.

2. That if any future treaty should be made with any other foreign power, in any articles either mentioned or not mentioned in the present Treaty, France shall be put on the same, or on as favourable terms as that power. And

3. That all the articles enumerated and specified in the tariff shall be admitted into this country on the duties, and with the stipulations stated in the sixth article.

He thus confined himself to the commercial part of the Treaty; nor was even all which belonged to that part, comprehended in the scope of these Resolutions. It would be necessary for the committee to take into their consideration the relative state of the two kingdoms. On the first blush of the matter, he believed he might venture to assert it, as a fact generally admitted, that France had the advantage in the gift of soil and climate, and in the amount of her natural produce; that, on the contrary, Great Britain was, on her part, as confessedly superior in her manufactures and artificial productions. Undoubtedly, in point of natural produce, France had greatly the advantage in this Treaty. Her wines, brandies, oils, and vinegars, particularly the two former articles, were matters of such important value in her produce, as greatly and completely to destroy all idea of reciprocity as to natural produce—we perhaps having nothing of that kind to put in competition, but simply the article of beer. But, on the contrary, was it not a fact as demonstrably clear, that Britain, in its turn, possessed some manufactures exclusively her own, and that in others she had so completely the advantage of her neighbour as to put competition at defiance? This then was the relative condition, and this the precise ground, on which it was imagined that a valuable correspondence and connexion between the two might be established. Having each its own and distinct staple—having each that which the other wanted; and not clashing in the great and leading lines of their respective riches, they were like two great traders in different branches, they might enter into a traffick which would prove mutually beneficial to them. Granting that a large quantity of their natural produce would be brought into this country, would any man say, that we should not send more cottons by the direct course now settled, than by the circuitous passages formerly used—more of our woollens, than while restricted in their importation to particular ports, and burthened under heavy duties? Would not more of our earthen ware, and other articles, which, under all the disadvantages that they formerly suffered, still, from their intrinsic superiority, force their way regularly into France, now be sent thither? and would not the aggregate of our manufactures be greatly and eminently benefited in going to this market loaded only with duties from twelve to ten, and in one instance with only five per cent? If the advantages in this respect were not so palpable and apparent as to strike and satisfy every mind interested in the business, would not the House have had very different petitions on their table than that presented this day? The fact was apparent. The article (sadlery) charged the most highly in the tariff, gave no sort of alarm. The traders in this article, though charged with a duty of fifteen per cent, knew their superiority so well, that they cheerfully embraced the condition, and conceived that the liberty would be highly advantageous to them. A market of so many millions of people—a market so near and prompt—a market of expeditious and certain return—of necessary and extensive consumption, thus added to the manufactures and commerce of Britain, was an object which we ought to look up to with eager and satisfied ambition. To procure this, we certainly ought not to scruple to give liberal conditions. We ought not to hesitate, because this, which must be so greatly advantageous to us, must also have its benefit for them. It was a great boon procured on easy terms, and as such we ought to view it. It was not merely a consoling, but an exhilarating speculation to the mind of an Englishman, that, after the empire had been engaged in a competition the most arduous and imminent of any that ever threatened a nation— after struggling for its existence, still it maintained its rank and efficacy so firmly, that France, finding they could not shake her, now opened its arms, and offered a beneficial connexion with her on easy, liberal, and advantageous terms.

We had agreed by this treaty to take from France, on small duties, the luxuries of her soil, which, however, the refinements of ourselves had converted into necessaries. The wines of France were already so much in the possession of our markets, that, with all the high duties paid by us, they found their way to our tables. Was it then a serious injury to admit these luxuries on easier terms? The admission of them would not supplant the wines of Portugal, nor of Spain, but would supplant only a useless and pernicious manufacture in this country. He stated the enormous increase of the import of French wines lately, and instanced the months of July and August, the two most unlikely months in the year, to show the increase of this trade. The committee would not then perceive any great evil in admitting this article on easy terms. The next was brandy, and here it would be inquired whether the diminution of duty was an eligible measure. He believed they would also agree with him on this article, when they viewed it with regard to smuggling. The reduction of the duties would have a material effect on the contraband in this article: it was certain that the legal importation bore no proportion to the quantity clandestinely imported; for the legal importation of brandy was no more than 600,000 gallons, and the supposed amount of the smuggled, at the most rational and best-founded estimate, was between three and four hundred thousand gallons. Seeing then that this article had taken such complete possession of the state of the nation, it might be right to procure to the State a greater advantage from the article than heretofore, and to crush the contraband by legalizing the market.

The oil and vinegar of France were comparatively small objects, but, like the former, they were luxuries which had taken the shape of necessaries, and which we could suffer nothing from accepting on easy terms. These were the natural produce of France to be admitted under this treaty. Their next inquiry should be to see if France had any manufactures peculiar to herself, or in which she so greatly excelled as to give us alarm on account of the Treaty, viewing it in that aspect. Cambric was the first which stared him in the face, but which, when he looked around him, and observed the general countenance of the committee, he could hardly think it necessary to detain them a moment upon. The fact was, it was an article in which our competition with France had ceased, and there was no injury in granting an easy importation to that which we would have at any rate. In no other article was there any thing very formidable in the rivalry of France. Glass would not be imported to any amount. In particular kinds of lace, indeed, they might have the advantage, but none which they would not enjoy independent of the treaty: and the clamours about millinery were vague and unmeaning, when, in addition to all these benefits, we included the richness of the country with which we were to trade: with its superior population of twenty millions to eight, and of course a proportionate consumption, together with its vicinity to us, and the advantages of quick and regular returns, who could hesitate for a moment to applaud the system, and look forward with ardour and impatience to its speedy ratification? The possession of so extensive and safe a market must improve our commerce, while the duties transferred from the hands of smugglers to their proper channel would benefit our revenue—the two sources of British opulence and British power.

Viewing the relative circumstances of the two countries then in this way, he saw no objection to the principle of the exchange of their respective commodities. He saw no objection to this, because he perceived and felt that our superiority in the tariff was manifest. The excellence of our manufactures was unrivalled, and in the operation must give the balance to England. But it was said, that the manufacturers dreaded the continuance of this superiority. They were alarmed at the idea of a competition with Ireland, and consequently they must be more under apprehensions at the idea of a rivalry with France. He always did think, and he must still continue to think, that the opinions of the manufacturers on this point were erroneous. They raised the clamour in respect to Ireland chiefly, he imagined, because they perceived no certain and positive advantage by the intercourse to counterbalance this precarious and uncertain evil. In this instance, their consent to the treaty did not proceed from a blind acquiescence, for they never would be blind to their interest; but now that they saw so certain and so valuable an advantage to be reaped, the benefits being no longer doubtful, they were willing to hazard the probability of the injury.

Some gentlemen thought proper to contend, that no beneficial treaty could be formed between this country and France, because no such treaty had ever been formed, and because, on the contrary, commercial intercourses with her had always been injurious to England. This reasoning was completely fallacious, though it sounded largely. For, in the first place, we had not, during a long series of years, experienced any commercial connexion with France, and could not therefore form a rational estimate of its merits; and secondly, though it might be true that a commercial intercourse founded on the treaty of Utrecht would have been injurious, it did not follow that this would prove the same; for at that time the manufactures, in which we now excelled, had hardly existence, but were on the side of France instead of being against her. The tariff did not then, as now, comprehend all the articles in which we comparatively excelled; but in addition to the produce of France, which at all periods must be the same, she had the balance of manufactures also in her favour. At that period also the prejudices of our manufacturers against France were in their rage, and corresponded with the party violence of the day in the reprobation of the measure; but so far was the Parliament from entertaining the opinion of no treaty being otherwise than detrimental, which could be made with France, that they went up with an address to her Majesty, praying her to renew commercial negociations with the Court of France. It was not correctly stated, neither, that we had invariably considered it as our policy to resist all connexion with France. She had been more jealous of us than we of her—Prohibitions began on the part of France, and we only retaliated in our own defence. These parts of his subject he felt it difficult to drop, without again adverting to the effect of this treaty on our revenue, which would almost exceed credibility, though it would cause an average reduction of 50*l.* per cent. in every article in our book of rates; on French wines the reduction would be 10,000*l.* per annum; on Portugal wines, 170,000*l.* should the Methuen Treaty be continued; and, on brandy, a reduction of 20,000*l.* The surrender of revenue for great commercial purposes was a policy by no means unknown in the history of Great Britain; but here we enjoyed the extraordinary advantage of having it returned to us in a three-fold rate, by extending and legalizing the importation of the articles. When it was considered that the increase must exceed the concession which we made, it would no longer be an argument that we cannot afford this reduction. Increase by means of reduction, he was obliged to confess, appeared once a paradox; but experience had now convinced us that it was more than practicable. *Parliamentary History*, Vol XXVI, col 383–9

_____

3 House of Lords Protest against the Enactment of the Corn Law of 1815

At the close of the Napoleonic Wars, the landed interests procured the enactment of the Corn Law of 1815, aimed at ensuring sufficient prices for agricultural products, and to protect the home producer from foreign competition. This measure passed into law with little difficulty, though there was some extra-parliamentary agitation against it. It prohibited the import of foreign foodstuffs until the price at home reached a high figure—80s per quarter for wheat. A formal protest against it was entered on the journals of the House of Lords and some of the points made in this protest anticipate the case against the Corn Laws made in the 1840s. The first four signatories are of particular interest: the Duke of Sussex (1773–1843) was the sixth son of King George III, and notable as a royal patron of many liberal causes; the Duke of Gloucester (1776–1834) was a nephew of King George III; Lords Grenville and Wellesley were important political figures; and Grenville (1759–1834) led one group of the Whig party, and had served as prime minister in 1806–7, as well as holding a variety of other important ministerial offices. The Marquis Wellesley (1760–1842) was the elder brother of the Duke of Wellington; he had been governor-general of India as well as holding important political offices at home. It can be seen then that free-trade ideas were by no means confined to economic writers by this time.

_____

Protest against the Corn Bill.] On the third reading of the Bill it was moved, "that this Bill be rejected;" which motion having, on a division, been negatived, the following Protest was entered:

"Dissentient,

"1. Because we are adverse in principle to all new restraints on commerce. We think it certain that public prosperity is best promoted, by leaving uncontrouled the free current of national industry; and we wish rather, by well-considered steps, to bring back our commercial legislation to the straight and simple line of wisdom, than to increase the deviation, by subjecting additional and extensive branches of the public interest to fresh systems of artificial and injurious restriction.

"2. Because we think that the great practical rule, of leaving all commerce unfettered, applies more peculiarly, and on still stronger grounds of justice as well as of policy, to the corn trade than to any other. Irresistible indeed must be that necessity which could, in our judgment, authorize the Legislature to tamper with the sustenance of the people, and to impede the free purchase and sale of that article, on which depends the existence of so large a portion of the community.

"3. Because we think that the expectations of ultimate benefit from this measure are founded on a delusive theory. We cannot persuade ourselves that this law will ever contribute to produce plenty, cheapness, or steadiness of price. So long as it operates at all, its effects must be the opposite of these. Monopoly is the parent of scarcity, of dearness, and of uncertainty. To cut off any of the sources of supply can only tend to lessen its abundance; to close against ourselves the cheapest market for any commodity, must enhance the price at which we purchase it; and to confine the consumer of corn to the produce of his own country, is to refuse to ourselves the benefit of that provision which Providence itself has made for equalizing to man the variations of season and of climate.

"4. But whatever may be the future consequences of this law, at some distant and uncertain period, we see, with pain, that these hopes must be purchased at the expense of a great and present evil. To compel the consumer to purchase corn dearer at home than it might be imported from abroad, is the immediate practical effect of this law. In this way alone can it operate. Its present protection, its promised extension of agriculture must result (if at all) from the profits which it creates by keeping up the price of corn to an artificial level. These future benefits are the consequences expected, but as we confidently believe erroneously expected, from giving a bounty to the grower of corn, by a tax levied on its consumer.

"5. Because we think that the adoption of any permanent law, for such a purpose, required the fullest and most laborious investigation. Nor would it have been sufficient for our satisfaction could we have been convinced of the general policy of so hazardous an experiment. A still further inquiry would have been necessary to persuade us that the present moment was fit for its adoption. In such an inquiry we must have had the means of satisfying ourselves what its immediate operation will be as connected with the various and pressing circumstances of public difficulty and distress with which the country is now surrounded; with the state of our circulation and currency; of our agriculture and manufactures; of our internal and external commerce; and above all with the condition and reward of the industrious and labouring classes of our community.

"On all these particulars, as they respect this question, we think that Parliament is almost wholly uninformed; on all we see reason for the utmost anxiety and alarm from the operation of this law.

"Lastly, Because if we could approve of the principle and purpose of this law, we think that no sufficient foundation has been laid for its details. The evidence before us, unsatisfactory and imperfect as it is, seems to us rather to disprove than to support the propriety of the high price adopted as the standard of importation, and the fallacious mode by which that price is to be ascertained.

"And on all these grounds we are anxious to record our dissent from a measure so precipitate in its course, and, as we fear, so injurious in its consequences.

AUGUSTUS FREDERICK (d. of Sussex),
WILLIAM FREDERICK (d. of Gloucester),
GRENVILLE,
WELLESLEY,
ESSEX,
TORRINGTON,
DUTTON (marquis of Douglas),
CHANDOS BUCKINGHAM,
MONTFORT,
KING,
CARLISLE.
Hansard's *Parliamentary Debates*, First Series, Vol XXX, col
263–5

4 Thomas Tooke The 1820 Petition of the London Merchants

The story of free trade in Britain, its rise and its fall, is be-
devilled by the polemical nature of much of the evidence to
be considered. An early example of this is provided by the
'Petition of the London Merchants' of 1820. Ostensibly the
product of a group of important commercial figures putting
forward the fruit of their own experiences and knowledge, it
was in fact drafted by Thomas Tooke. Tooke (1774–1858) was
an associate of Ricardo and Huskisson, one of the founders of
the Political Economy Club, and a prolific writer on economic
questions. He was not, however, a London merchant.

To the Honourable the Commons of Great Britain and Ire-
    land:—
The Petition of, etc.
Humbly showeth,
    That foreign commerce is eminently conducive to the wealth
and prosperity of a country, by enabling it to import the commodities for the production of which the soil, climate, capital,
and industry of other countries are best calculated, and to export

D

in payment those articles for which its own situation is better adapted.

That freedom from restraint is calculated to give the utmost extension to foreign trade, and the best direction to the capital and industry of the country.

That the maxim of buying in the cheapest market, and selling in the dearest, which regulates every merchant in his individual dealings, is strictly applicable as the best rule for the trade of the whole nation.

That a policy founded on these principles would render the commerce of the world an interchange of mutual advantages, and diffuse an increase of wealth and enjoyments among the inhabitants of each State.

That, unfortunately, a policy the very reverse of this has been, and is, more or less, adopted and acted upon by the Government of this and of every other country, each trying to exclude the productions of other countries, with the specious and well-meant design of encouraging its own productions, thus inflicting on the bulk of its subjects who are consumers, the necessity of submitting to privations in the quantity or quality of commodities, and thus rendering what ought to be the source of mutual benefit and of harmony among States, a constantly-recurring occasion of jealousy and hostility.

That the prevailing prejudices in favour of the protective or restrictive system may be traced to the erroneous supposition that every importation of foreign commodities occasions a diminution or discouragement of our own productions to the same extent, whereas it may be clearly shown that although the particular description of production which could not stand against unrestrained foreign competition would be discouraged, yet, as no importation could be continued for any length of time without a corresponding exportation, direct or indirect, there would be an encouragement, for the purpose of that exportation, of some other production to which our situation might be better suited, thus affording at least an equal, and probably a greater, and certainly a more beneficial employment to our own capital and labour.

That, of the numerous protective and prohibitory duties of our commercial code, it may be proved, that while all operate as a very heavy tax on the community at large, very few are of any ultimate benefit to the classes in whose favour they were originally instituted, and none to the extent of the loss occasioned by them to other classes.

That, among the other evils of the restrictive or protective system, not the least is, that the artificial protection of one branch of industry, or source of production, against foreign competition, is set up as a ground of claim by other branches for similar protection, so that if the reasoning upon which these restrictive or prohibitory regulations are founded were followed out consistently, it would not stop short of excluding us from all foreign commerce whatsoever. And the same train of argument, which, with corresponding prohibitions and protective duties, should exclude us from foreign trade, might be brought forward to justify the re-enactment of restrictions upon the interchange of productions (unconnected with public revenue) among the kingdoms composing the union, or among the counties of the same kingdom.

That an investigation of the effects of the restrictive system, at this time, is peculiarly called for, as it may, in the opinion of your petitioners, lead to a strong presumption that the distress which now so generally prevails is considerably aggravated by that system, and that some relief may be obtained by the earliest practicable removal of such of the restraints as may be shown to be most injurious to the capital and industry of the community, and to be attended with no compensating benefit to the public revenue.

That a declaration against the anti-commercial principles of our restrictive system is of the more importance at the present juncture inasmuch as, in several instances of recent occurrence, the merchants and manufacturers in foreign States have assailed their respective Governments with applications for further protective or prohibitory duties and regulations, urging the example and authority of this country, against which they are almost exclusively directed, as a sanction for the policy of such measures. And certainly, if the reasoning upon which our restrictions have been defended is worth anything, it will apply in behalf of the regulations of foreign States against us. They insist upon our superiority in capital and machinery, as we do upon their comparative exemption from taxation, and with equal foundation.

That nothing would more tend to counteract the commercial hostility of foreign States than the adoption of a more enlightened and more conciliatory policy on the part of this country.

That although, as a matter of mere diplomacy, it may sometimes answer to hold out the removal of particular prohibitions, or high duties, as depending upon corresponding concessions by other States in our favour, it does not follow that we should maintain our restrictions in cases where the desired concessions on their part cannot be obtained. Our restrictions would not be the less prejudicial to our capital and industry because other Governments persisted in preserving impolitic regulations.

That, upon the whole, the most liberal would prove to be the most politic course on such occasions.

That, independent of the direct benefit to be derived by this country on every occasion of such concession or relaxation, a great incidental object would be gained by the recognition of a sound principle or standard to which all subsequent arrangements might be referred, and by the salutary influence which a promulgation of such just views by the legislature, and by the nation at large, could not fail to have on the policy of other States.

That in thus declaring, as your petitioners do, their conviction of the impolicy and injustice of the restrictive system, and in desiring every practicable relaxation of it, they have in view only such parts of it as are not connected, or are only subordinately so, with the public revenue. As long as the necessity for the present amount of revenue subsists, your petitioners cannot expect so important a branch of it as the Customs to be given up, nor to be materially diminished, unless some substitute, less objectionable, be suggested. But it is against every restrictive regulation of trade, not essential to the revenue—against all duties merely protective from foreign competition—and against the excess of such duties as are partly for the purpose of revenue and partly for that of protection, that the prayer of the present petition is respectfully submitted to the wisdom of Parliament.

Your petitioners therefore humbly pray that your honourable house will be pleased to take the subject into consideration, and to adopt such measures as may be calculated to give greater freedom to foreign commerce, and thereby to increase the resources of the State.

The 1820 Petition of the London Merchants, drafted by Thomas Tooke.

5 William Huskisson   Speech in Parliament

William Huskisson (1770–1830) can be seen as Pitt's successor in the line of statesmen who translated free-trade ideas into practical measures. As President of the Board of Trade in Lord Liverpool's government between 1823 and 1827 he reduced Britain's import duties and greatly modified the Navigation Acts which protected British shipping from foreign competition. In 1827–8 his proposals for modifications in the Corn Laws provoked serious disagreements in the Tory party, and the measure which eventually struggled to the statute book in 1828 was an unsatisfactory compromise between the liberal views of Huskisson and the protectionist attitudes of Wellington and other right-wingers. The excerpt from a speech by Huskisson in 1828, given here, shows the difficulties surrounding the question of agricultural protection, where economic argument was complicated by the fact that the landowners were the dominant influence in the country's social and political life.

—The hon. and learned member for Kircudbright (Mr. Fergusson) was one of those who insisted on some law which should keep up the price of barley and oats. But did the hon. and learned member forget, that in the last year those grains had received a

considerable advance on the scale proposed? The hon. member
forgot that the central point of oats had been advanced from 21s.
to 25s., and that of barley from 30s. to 33s.; no corresponding
advance being made upon the article of wheat. He was surprised
that the hon. and learned member should overlook this point;
and that he should not see that 25s. was a higher ratio for oats
than 60s. was for wheat. He had looked carefully back to the
prices of former years; and he found no instance in which the
price at which importation should be permitted had been fixed
so high as 25s. The hon. and learned member seemed to think,
too, that there was no difference between the scale of duties now
proposed, and the amendment moved by the hon. member for
Dorsetshire last year. This impression was a mistaken one. The
object of the last year's amendment of the hon. member for
Dorsetshire had been to raise the pivot price of wheat from 60s.
to 64s., but to leave the graduations of the scale, both in the
ascent and descent of the duty, as it stood; but it was clear, upon
the slightest calculation, that, from the beginning to the end of
the scale, that change went to make a most important difference.
—The hon. member for Bridgenorth had announced his hostility
to the resolutions proposed, and his intention to suggest new
ones. It would have been as well, he thought, if the hon. member
had brought forward his resolutions at once. In fairness, both to
the House and to the country, he thought that hon. members who
had counter-resolutions to propose, would have done well to have
named them on that evening, that they might have gone forth
side by side with those of ministers for general consideration. In
this there could neither have been any thing objectionable, nor
any needless occupation of time: and ministers, if they were not
immediately to have the benefit of hon. gentlemen's speeches,
might yet have had the advantage of seeing, and perhaps deriving
instruction from their plans. The hon. member for Bridgenorth
approved neither of the existing law, it appeared, nor of that
proposed: for he said, that if the President of the Board of Trade
had brought forward the system of the last year *ipsissimis verbis*,
he would have objected to it. The hon. member then complained

that the system now proposed was of too complicated a character. Now, he could not see that it was more complicated than that of the last year. The scheme now proposed took the two extremes of the scale as it was formed for the last year, and proposed to enact such regulations as, at the price of 70s., should let in wheat at a merely nominal duty, and, on the contrary, at the price of 60s. should pretty nearly prevent its admission altogether. That was an equitable arrangement, and one which could lead to no inconvenience. When corn was either much wanted here, or at a very low price abroad, it would certainly find its way into the country. Let the House look, however, to what had occurred since last year. It was said that after the bill of last year had received amendment in another place, which materially altered its effect—it was said, that in any reconsideration of the subject in a future session, the House ought to proceed with a view to what the result of that bill had been in experience. He agreed with his right hon. friend, that that experience had received more consideration than it deserved: five hundred thousand quarters of wheat, however, had come in when the duty exceeded 20s.; therefore there was a *prima facie* case made out, that 20s. was not a sufficient duty to exclude. This fact, then, in the construction of the present measure, had been considered; and it was upon that ground that an attempt was contemplated, without departing from the principle of the last year's bill, or sacrificing any of the views which it had embraced, to quiet the apprehension which had arisen out of the importation at a 20s. duty, and to throw an additional drag or impediment in the way by which foreign corn, in a given state of the market, was to be admitted. All parties last year had been agreed upon the mischief which would arise from permitting large importations of foreign wheat, when the price in the home market was between 60s. and 64s. The measure of the present year was calculated to check such importation: it was no deviation from the principle of the last year's bill, or from the manner in which that bill dealt with the subject; but it was so constructed, as to defeat a possible course, which it was generally agreed, if put in execution, would prove inconvenient. He admitted fully that, in the course of the last year, there had been circumstances calculated to produce a larger importation, at given rates of duty, than was likely to occur again. In the first place, the act of November, 1826, had given the Crown the power to admit five hundred thousand quarters of foreign wheat at 12s. a quarter duty. That power, it was true, had not been exerted, for the occasion for its exercise had not arisen; but the belief that it would be called into effect, and the contemplation of further changes, had brought a large supply of foreign corn into the warehouses of the country—a larger quantity, probably, than would otherwise have been introduced. The expectation of the admission of the five hundred thousand quarters at 12s. duty had failed; and the general measure, upon which something had perhaps been calculated, had been defeated in another place; and a short time was open to get rid of a large supply of a commodity which received no benefit from keeping. The result was, that a sort of panic had seized upon the holders of foreign corn in bond, which had produced considerable loss; it had been taken out of bond at high rates of duty, and rapidly forced into consumption. It was necessary, therefore, in any estimate of what had arisen under the last year's law, to consider these circumstances. But the right hon. President of the Board of Trade had stated truly, that it was their duty, as practical men, to look at the measure of the present session as one which was to settle what the rule and what the law was, by which all the transactions of the country relating to the land were to be regulated. The question was one, the final adjustment of which was not merely deeply desirable, but a matter of paramount necessity; for it was one by which all acts and business of men's lives were influenced and governed. The object of the House should be, to pass a measure which men might believe, and look upon to be, a lasting and a conclusive one;—an award, if he might be allowed the expression, between the exaggerated prejudices entertained against all freedom on the one side, and the exaggerated hopes which might have been conceived by the other;—a measure which, if it was not the very best which could be introduced, might yet be one which would prove an adjustment of the question so long agitated with so much inconvenience to society;—a question, one of the worst effects of the uncertainty of which was, that some particular class of the community was constantly apprehending that its interests were about to be sacrificed to those of another class; while the duty of the House, as well as its real disposition, was to look upon all interests impartially. It was for purposes, and with feelings of this description, that the present measure had been submitted to the House. He did not think it the best which might have been brought forward; but he did believe that it was a measure, when duly considered, which, with reference to all the circumstances of the currency, and the state of public feeling, was more likely to abate those angry squabbles which the absence of final measures had given rise to, than any other which, in the present condition of the country, could be introduced. As to those who objected to it on the score that the interests of agriculture were not sufficiently protected, he had already briefly replied to their observations. The hon. member for Somersetshire professed himself pleased with the law of 1815. He could only say to that hon. member, that he lamented from the bottom of his soul, the mass of evil and misery, and destruction of capital, which that law, in the course of its twelve years' operation, had produced: and he did believe that he could make it distinctly appear, if the moment were a proper one, that the effect of the bill, as far as regarded the agriculturists themselves, had been to keep the prices of produce lower, for those twelve years, than they would have been, even if the trade in corn had been entirely open. Hansard's *Parliamentary Debates*, Second Series, Vol XVIII, col 1395–8, 31 March 1828

---

6 J. R. McCulloch Statistical Account of the British Empire

J. R. McCulloch (1789–1864) was professor of political economy at London University from 1828 to 1832, and was regarded as one of the leading economists and statisticians of

his day. His *Principles of Political Economy* (1825) was one of the
best-known contemporary textbooks on the subject, and he
wrote a number of other books and many articles on economic
questions. The passage cited here is a good example of the
dominant contemporary economic view of free trade and
protection.

The absence of monopolies, and the non-interference of the
government in industrious undertakings, undoubtedly conduce
in no ordinary degree to the progress of industry. Every man is
always exerting himself to find out how he may best extend his
command over the necessaries and conveniences of life; and
sound policy requires that he should, so long as he does not
interfere with the rights and privileges of others, be allowed to
pursue his own interest in his own way. Human reason is, no
doubt, limited and fallible; we are often swayed by prejudices,
and are apt to be deceived by appearances: still, however, it is
certain that the desire to promote our own purposes contributes
far more than any thing else to render us clear-sighted and
sagacious.—"*Nul sentiment dans l'homme ne tient son intelligence
éveillée autant que l'intérêt personnel. Il donne de l'esprit aux plus simples.*"
The principle that individuals are, generally speaking, the best
judges of what is most beneficial for themselves, is now universally
admitted to be the only one that can be safely relied on. No
writer of authority has, latterly, ventured to maintain the ex-
ploded and untenable doctrine, that governments may advan-
tageously interfere to regulate the pursuits of their subjects. It is
their duty to preserve order; to prevent one from injuring
another; to maintain, in short, the equal rights and privileges of
all. But it is not possible for them to go one step further, without
receding from the principle of non-interference, and laying themselves open to the charge of acting partially by some, and unjustly
by others.

The most comprehensive experience corroborates the truth of
these remarks. The natural order of things has been less interfered
with in Great Britain than in most other countries. Since the

passing of the famous act of James I., in 1624, for the abolition of monopolies, full scope has been given to the competition of the home producers; and, though the various resources of talent and genius have not been so fully, perhaps, or at least so early, developed as they would have been had there been no restrictions on our intercourse with foreigners, they have been stimulated in a degree unknown in most other countries. France, previously to the Revolution, was divided into provinces, having each peculiar privileges, and separate codes of revenue laws; and in consequence the intercourse between them was subjected to the most oppressive restrictions. In Germany and Spain the same miserable system prevailed; so that they were not only deprived of the freedom of foreign, but even of internal, commerce. The inhabitants of each province being in a great measure isolated from the rest, there was comparatively little competition; and, instead of invention and active exertion, there was nothing but routine and sluggish indifference. Holland and the United States have been almost the only countries that have enjoyed the same degree of internal freedom as Great Britain; and the former, notwithstanding the unfavourable physical circumstances under which she is placed, has long been, and still is, the richest country in Europe; while the latter, whose condition is in other respects more favourable, is advancing with giant steps in the career of improvement.

It is sometimes said, that restrictions on industry and commerce cannot be so injurious as has been represented, seeing the progress we have made notwithstanding they have always existed amongst us. The previous details show the weight to be attached to this allegation. The restrictions referred to have been confined to some branches of foreign trade: and, luckily, the freedom allowed to all sorts of industry at home would have insured our advance though the fetters laid on foreign trade had been a good deal more oppressive than they actually have been. But to imagine, as many have done, that these restrictions contributed to accelerate our progress, is the climax of absurdity. Their influence has, in every case, been distinctly and completely the reverse; but, though considerable, it has been insufficient to countervail the advantages resulting from the freedom we otherwise enjoyed. J. R. McCulloch. *Statistical Account of the British Empire*, Vol II, pp 36–7, London, 1837.

PART TWO

The Victory of Free Trade—the Corn Laws and the League

The repeal of the Corn Laws in the 1840s settled the commercial policy of Britain for the greater part of a century. A leading part in the fight for repeal was taken by the Anti-Corn Law League, which developed out of the Manchester Anti-Corn Law Association, founded in September 1838. Manchester throughout provided the main centre and many of the leading spirits of this agitation against the Corn Laws. An early success of the Manchester free traders was won when an anti-corn law petition was forced through the Manchester Chamber of Commerce (7) against considerable opposition.

Arguments for Free Trade came from a variety of sources, including official agencies. A favourite source was the Report of the Select Committee on Import Duties (8). This committee was appointed by the House of Commons in 1840 at the instance of Joseph Hume, a radical MP, and manipulated skilfully to produce a case against protection.

The growth of the League owed much to the skill of its leaders, and especially to Richard Cobden (1804–65). He had a clear and practical style of speaking and writing, as well as great gifts as an organiser. Two examples of his speeches are cited here, one delivered in the House of Commons (9), the other before a great meeting in the Free Trade Hall, Manchester (10).

The crusade against the Corn Laws, however, did not depend only on the exposition of economic theories or the skilful persuasion of men like Cobden and John Bright (1811–89). The Anti-Corn Law League developed into a well-organised and sophisticated political machine. Clever propaganda, and a good deal of unscrupulous machination, kept the question in the public eye. The documents 11–14 give a small selection of material relating to these activities. The Corn Laws also came under fire from other directions; although Chartism and the League were rivals rather than allies, anti-Corn Law feeling also existed in Chartist circles (15).

The League led the fight against agricultural protection. Founded in 1839, it was only in the 1840s that it made much headway; but by 1845 it had a large and complex organisation and a great deal of money. Nevertheless, it was never to be within measurable distance of real power in a society in which a ruling minority was deeply entrenched. The great Conservative and Whig groupings controlled Parliament, and Free Trade could only come when one of them was willing to enact it. In the years 1841–5 both major parties moved towards more liberal commercial policies. Peel was the key figure; his great budgets of 1842 and 1845 cut existing duties, and the satisfactory results of this policy paved the way for the final decision to repeal the Corn Laws. A budget speech of 1845 (16) shows the way in which Peel's mind was working. In his Edinburgh Letter of the same year (17) Lord John Russell brought the Whigs into line against the Corn Laws. The final crisis was precipitated by the Irish famine. Peel determined to use this occasion to repeal the Corn Laws, and Peelite and Whig votes were mainly responsible for doing so in 1846, while the League's growling out of doors maintained the pressure. Peel's party was split by his decision and he was thrown out of office.

In his resignation speech (18) Peel justified his policy by an emotional appeal which, while it widened his split with the protectionists, lent a romantic air to Free Trade in future years. This section ends (19) with the unavailing protest of the protectionist peers against the passage of the repeal measure through the House of Lords. With the end of the Corn Laws, the fight for Free Trade was largely won. The next few years were to see the dismantling of the rest of the old protectionist system; by 1852 all major political groups had accepted Free Trade as the corner-stone of Britain's commercial policies.

7 A. Prentice   History of the Anti-Corn Law League

The 1838 Petition of the Manchester Chamber of Commerce. At a meeting of the Chamber on 20 December 1838, its Free Trade members, headed by Cobden, insisted in pushing through a strong petition against the Corn Laws. Even in Manchester, however, there was opposition to such an un-equivocal stand, and the action of the Free Traders caused a split in the Chamber, its more conservative wing, which included some of the most influential members, seceding to form a separate Manchester Commercial Association. The two bodies did not come together again until Free Trade had won the day.

To the Honourable the Commons of Great Britain and Ireland, in Parliament assembled:—

The Petition of the President, Vice-President, Directors, and Members of the Chamber of Commerce and Manufactures of Manchester, agreed to in a Special General Meeting, held on the 20th day of December, 1838,

Humbly showeth,

That your petitioners deem it their imperative duty to call the immediate attention of your honourable house to the consideration of the existing laws affecting the free importation of food.

That your petitioners would premise that you are already acquainted with the nature and extent of the cotton trade; combining, as it does, a larger amount of capital, with greater enterprise and skill, and giving more extensive and better regulated employment than any other branch of manufacturing industry. This source of increasing population and wealth, which is now become essential to our well-being as a nation, owes no sort of allegiance to the soil of England; and if it has grown up with a rapidity unparalleled in the annals of trade, history affords us many examples to show how speedily it may, by misgovernment, be banished to other shores.

That your petitioners view, with great alarm, the rapid extension of foreign manufactures, and they have, in particular, to deplore the consequent diminution of a profitable trade with the Continent of Europe; to which, notwithstanding the great increase in population since the termination of the war, the exports have been actually less in value during the last five years than they were during the first five years after the peace, and whilst the demand for all those articles, in which the greatest amount of the labour of our artisans is comprised, has been constantly diminishing, the exportation of the raw material has been as rapidly increasing.

That several nations of the Continent not only produce sufficient manufactures for their own consumption, but they successfully compete with us in neutral foreign markets. Amongst other instances that might be given to show the formidable growth of the cotton manufacture abroad, is that of the cotton hosiery of Saxony, of which, owing to its superior cheapness, nearly four times as much is exported, as from this country; the Saxons exporting annually to the United States of America alone, a quantity equal to the exports from England to all parts of the world; whilst the still more important fact remains to be adduced, that Saxon hose, manufactured from English yarn, after paying a duty of 20 per cent., are beginning to be introduced into this country and sold for home consumption, at lower prices than they can be produced for by our manufacturers.

That further proof of the rapid progress in manufacturing industry going on upon the Continent is afforded in the fact that establishments for the making of all kinds of machinery for spinning and weaving cotton, flax, and wool, have lately been formed in nearly all the large towns of Europe, in which English skilled artisans are at the present moment diligently employed in teaching the native mechanics to make machines, copied from models of the newest invention of this country, and not a week passes in which individuals of the same valuable class do not quit the workshops of Manchester, Leeds, and Birmingham, to enter upon similar engagements abroad.

That the superiority we have hitherto possessed in our un-rivalled roads and canals is no longer peculiar to this country. Railroads to a great extent, and at a less cost than in England, are proceeding in all parts of Europe and the United States of America, whilst, from the want of profitable investment at home, capital is constantly seeking employment in foreign countries; and thus supplying the greatest deficiency under which our rivals previously laboured.

That whilst calling the attention of your honourable house to facts calculated to excite the utmost alarm for the well-being of our manufacturing prosperity, your Petitioners cannot too earnestly make known that the evils are occasioned by our im-politic and unjust legislation, which, by preventing the British manufacturer from exchanging the produce of his labour for the corn of other countries, enables our foreign rivals to purchase their food at one half the price at which it is sold in this market; and your petitioners declare it to be their solemn conviction, that this is the commencement only of a state of things which, unless arrested by a timely repeal of all protective duties upon the importation of corn and of all foreign articles of subsistence, must eventually transfer our manufacturing industry into other and rival countries.

That deeply impressed with such apprehensions, your peti-tioners cannot look with indifference upon, nor conceal from your honourable house the perilous condition of those surround-ing multitudes, whose subsistence from day to day depends upon the prosperity of the cotton trade. Already the million have raised the cry for food. Reason, compassion, and sound policy demand that the excited passions be allayed, otherwise evil con-sequences may ensue. The continuance of the loyal attachment of the people to the established institutions of the country can

E

never be permanently secured on any other grounds than those of universal justice. Holding one of these eternal principles to be the unalienable right of every man, freely to exchange the results of his labour for the productions of other people, and maintaining the practice of protecting one part of the community at the expense of all other classes, to be unsound and unjustifiable, your petitioners earnestly implore your honourable house to repeal all laws relating to the importation of foreign corn and other foreign articles of subsistence, and to carry out to the fullest extent, both as affects agriculture and manufactures, the true and peaceful principles of free trade, by removing all existing obstacles to the unrestricted employment of industry and capital. A. Prentice. *History of the Anti-Corn Law League*, 2nd ed, Vol I, pp 85–7, 1968

8 Import Duties Committee, 1840   Report

Import Duties Committee, 1840. This Report was for long a major source of argument and evidence in favour of Free Trade. The Select Committee was obtained, and largely managed, by Joseph Hume, a prominent radical MP and Free Trader. Its Report was reprinted in 1841 and 1842 and reissued, significantly enough, when the issue of Tariff Reform was again raised in 1903. It has long been accepted that the Report was no objective and impartial document. Even at the time, doubts were expressed on the reliability of some of the evidence accepted by the Committee, and subsequent work has shown that the Report was based on patchy and partisan information. This bias was due not only to the attitude of Hume and the other Free Traders on the Select Committee itself, but also to a group of key officials from the Board of Trade, who played an important role in the enquiry. The conception of a non-political and unbiased Civil Service had as yet scarcely emerged, and three leading officials gave free rein to their own Free Trade predilections. These were J. D. Hume (1774–1842), who was just completing twelve years as one of the joint secretaries to the Board of Trade; John Mac-

Gregor (1797–1857), who obtained the same office in 1840, and who later founded an unsound bank; and G. R. Porter (1792–1852), who had formed the Board of Trade's statistical department in 1834, and became joint secretary to the Board in 1841. The Free Trade bias of this trio was not confined to the 1840 Committee; they co-operated with the League, even to the extent of passing confidential government information to Cobden to be used against the government's commercial policies.

The Tariff of the United Kingdom presents neither congruity nor unity of purpose; no general principles seem to have been applied.

The Schedule to the Act 3 & 4 Will. 4, c. 56, for consolidating the Customs Duties, enumerates no fewer than 1,150 different rates of duty chargeable on imported articles, all other commodities paying duty as unenumerated; and very few of such rates appear to have been determined by any recognised standard; and it would be difficult for any person unacquainted with the details of the Tariff to estimate the probable amount of duty to which any given commodity would be found subjected. There are cases where the duties levied are simple and comprehensive; others, where they fall into details both vexatious and embarrassing.

The Tariff often aims at incompatible ends; the duties are sometimes meant to be both productive of revenue and for protective objects, which are frequently inconsistent with each other; hence they sometimes operate to the complete exclusion of foreign produce, and in so far no revenue can of course be received; and sometimes, when the duty is inordinately high, the amount of revenue becomes in consequence trifling. They do not make the receipt of revenue the main consideration, but allow that primary object of fiscal regulations to be thwarted by an attempt to protect a great variety of particular interests, at the expense of the revenue, and of the commercial intercourse with other countries. . . .

... Your Committee cannot refrain from impressing strongly on the attention of The House that the effect of prohibitory duties, while they are of course wholly unproductive to the revenue, is to impose an indirect tax on the consumer, often equal to the whole difference of price between the British article and the foreign article which the prohibition excludes. This fact has been strongly and emphatically urged on Your Committee by several witnesses; and the enormous extent of taxation so levied cannot fail to awaken the attention of The House. On articles of food alone, it is averred, according to the testimony laid before the Committee, that the amount taken from the consumer exceeds the amount of all the other taxes which are levied by the Government. And the witnesses concur in the opinion that the sacrifices of the community are not confined to the loss of revenue, but that they are accompanied by injurious effects upon wages and capital; they diminish greatly the productive powers of the country, and limit our active trading relations.

Somewhat similar is the action of high and protective duties. These impose upon the consumer a tax equal to the amount of the duties levied upon the foreign article, whilst it also increases the price of all the competing home-produced articles to the same amount as the duty; but that increased price goes, not to the Treasury, but to the protected manufacturer. It is obvious that high protective duties check importation, and consequently, are unproductive to the revenue; and experience shows, that the profit to the trader, the benefit to the consumer, and the fiscal interests of the country, are all sacrificed when heavy import duties impede the interchange of commodities with other nations.

The inquiries of Your Committee have naturally led them to investigate the effects of the protective system on manufacture and labour. They find on the part of those who are connected with some of the most important of our manufactures, a conviction, and a growing conviction, that the protective system is not, on the whole, beneficial to the protected manufactures themselves. Several witnesses have expressed the utmost willingness to surrender any protection they have from the Tariffs, and disclaim any benefit resulting from that protection; and Your Committee, in investigating the subject as to the amount of duties levied on the plea of protection to British manufactures, have to report that the amount does not exceed half a million sterling; and some of the manufacturers, who are supposed to be most interested in retaining those duties, are quite willing they should be abolished, for the purpose of introducing a more liberal system into our commercial policy.

Your Committee gather from the evidence that has been laid before them, that while the prosperity of our own manufactures is not to be traced to benefits derived from the exclusion of foreign rival manufacturers, so neither is the competition of continental manufacturers to be traced to a protective system. They are told that the most vigorous and successful of the manufactures on the Continent have grown, not out of peculiar favour shown to them by legislation, but from those natural and spontaneous advantages which are associated with labour and capital in certain localities, and which cannot be transferred elsewhere at the mandate of the Legislature, or at the will of the manufacturer. Your Committee see reason to believe, that the most prosperous fabrics are those which flourish without the aid of special favours. It has been stated to Your Committee, that the Legislation of Great Britain, whenever it is hostile to the introduction of foreign commodities, is invariably urged by the foreign states that produce such commodities, as a ground and a sanction for laws being passed by them hostile to the introduction of products of British industry; and while on the one hand, there is reason to believe that the liberalizing the Tariffs of Great Britain would lead to similar favourable changes in the tariffs of other nations, so it is seriously to be apprehended that a persistence in our illiberal and exclusive policy will bring with it increased imposts on, if not prohibitions against, the products of British labour being admitted to other countries.

With reference to the influence of the protective system upon wages, and on the condition of the labourer, Your Committee have to observe, that as the pressure of foreign competition is heaviest on those articles in the production of which the rate of wages is lowest, so it is obvious, in a country exporting so largely as England does, that other advantages may more than compensate for an apparent advantage in the money price of labour. The countries in which the rate of wages is lowest are not always those which manufacture most successfully; and Your Committee are persuaded that the best service that could be rendered to the industrious classes of the community, would be to extend the field of labour, and of demand for labour, by an extension of our commerce; and that the supplanting the present system of protection and prohibition, by a moderate Tariff, would encourage and multiply most beneficially for the State and for the people our commercial transactions.

Your Committee further recommend, that as speedily as possible the whole system of differential duties and of all restrictions should be reconsidered, and that a change therein be effected in such a manner that existing interests may suffer as little as possible in the transition to a more liberal and equitable state of things. Your Committee is persuaded that the difficulties of modifying the discriminating duties which favour the introduction of British colonial articles would be very much abated if the Colonies were themselves allowed the benefits of free trade with all the world.

The simplification they recommend would not only vastly facilitate the transactions of commerce, and thereby benefit the revenue, but would at the same time greatly diminish the cost of collection, remove multitudinous sources of complaint and vexation, and give an example to the world at large, which, emanating from a community distinguished above all others for its capital, its enterprise, its intelligence, and the extent of its trading relations, could not but produce the happiest effects; and consolidate the great interests of peace and commerce by associating them intimately and permanently with the prosperity of the whole family of nations. *Reports of Select Committees*, 601 of 1840

9 Richard Cobden   Speech in Parliament

Cobden in the House of Commons, 15 May 1843. He was
supporting an anti-Corn Law resolution moved by C. P.
Villiers, MP for Wolverhampton and an early champion of
Free Trade in the House of Commons. Villiers (1802–98) had
an aristocratic background, and his long tenure of the Wolver-
hampton constituency is instructive; he sat as MP for that
manufacturing town from 1835 till 1898!

This excerpt illustrates the clarity and cogency of Cobden's
style; there are none of the more florid techniques that Bright,
for instance, frequently employed, but a very skilful simplicity
which earned for Cobden a place on the roll of great Parliamentary figures. It was a style well suited to the intimate
atmosphere of the House of Commons.

. . . although we have had five nights' debate, the question
proposed by the hon. Member for Wolverhampton has been
scarcely touched, that is, how far you are justified in maintaining
a law, which restricts the supply of food to the people of this
country. In supporting the present Corn-law, you support a law
which inflicts scarcity on the people. You do that, or you do
nothing. You cannot operate in any way by this law, but by
inflicting scarcity on the people. Entertain that proposition, and
you cannot escape it, and if it is true, how many of you will dare
to vote for the continuance of the present law? You cannot
enhance the price of corn, or any other article, but by restricting
the supply. Are you justified in doing this, for the purpose of
raising your prices? . . .

. . . I want the Anti Corn-law League to be known as the Free
Trade League. I know that hon. Gentlemen opposite think that
all we want to do is to take away the corn monopoly. The public
mind is urged on by us against that key-stone in the arch of
monopoly; but I can tell hon. Gentlemen opposite, that that
organization never will be dispersed until there is a total abroga-
tion of every monopoly. There has been a great deal of talk of

free trade being theoretically, and in the abstract, right. Does the right hon. Gentleman know what that would lead to? If free trade be theoretically right—if it is as old as truth itself, why is it not applicable to the state and circumstances of this country? What! truth not applicable; then there must be something very false in your system, if truth cannot harmonise with it. Our object is to make you conform to truth, by making you dispense with your monopolies, and bringing your legislation within the bounds of justice. I thank you for the admission that we have a true cause, and armed with the truth of that cause I appeal to the friends of humanity, I appeal to those on the other side who profess and practise benevolence, I appeal to certain Members on the other side of the House, and I appeal especially to a certain noble Lord (Lord Ashley), and I ask him can he carry out his schemes of benevolence if he votes for any restriction on the supply of the people's food. If he should vote against the present motion, I ask him, will not he and his friends be viewed with suspicion in the manufacturing districts? We often hear a great deal about charity, but what have we to do with charity? Yes, I say, what have we to do with charity in this House? The people ask for justice and not charity. We are bound to deal out justice; how can charity be dealt out to an entire nation? Where a nation were the recipients it were difficult to imagine who could be the donors. I, therefore, exhort the advocates of religion, the advocates of education, the friends of moral and physical improvement, to reflect upon the votes which they are about to give. I ask, what will the country say if such Members, patching up a measure of detail, are found voting in the approaching division against the motion of the hon. Member for Wolver-hampton? I call upon them, therefore, to separate themselves from those with whom they are accustomed to act, unless they are prepared to lose all the influence which they have laboured so hard to acquire in the manufacturing districts. I call upon them to support the present measure if they hope to be useful. There are 7,000,000 or 8,000,000 of people without wheaten bread. If the people continue to descend in the scale of physical comfort, and to eat potatoes, the hope of moral improvement which the friends of humanity indulge, must be altogether disappointed. The right hon. Gentleman the President of the Board of Trade said, that the importation of 600,000 quarters of wheat would be a national calamity; but how otherwise are the people to be supported? *Parliamentary Debates*, Third Series, Vol LXIX, col 386 et seq

---

10 Richard Cobden   Speech in Manchester

Cobden speaking in the Free Trade Hall, Manchester, 15 January 1846. The next few documents (11–14) illustrate the various techniques and devices used by the Anti-Corn Law League to arouse support for its crusade. Some of these devices were not very creditable, and it is important to realise that for Cobden and some of the other leaders of the League the conflict was not just an argument about customs duties, but the attempt to create a world of peace and prosperity, with the nations linked in economic interdependence. It was not an ignoble vision, even if most of the League's supporters had narrower and more interested motives.

This speech was delivered to a great meeting in the Free Trade Hall, which the League had built. The final crisis over the Corn Laws was at hand, and so great was the interest that the seats in the Hall had been removed to enable more people to crowd in to hear the speeches.

I have never taken a limited view of the object or scope of this great principle. I have never advocated this question very much as a trader.

But I have been accused of looking too much to material interests. Nevertheless, I can say that I have taken as large and great a view of the effects of this mighty principle as ever did any man who dreamt over it in his own study. I believe that the physical gain will be the smallest gain to humanity from the success of this principle. I look farther; I see in the Free Trade principle that which shall act on the moral world as the principle of gravitation in the universe—drawing men together, thrusting aside the antagonism of race, and creed, and language, and uniting us in the bonds of eternal peace. I have looked even farther. I have speculated, and probably dreamt, in the dim future—ay, a thousand years hence—I have speculated on what the effect of the triumph of this principle may be. I believe that the effect will be to change the face of the world, so as to introduce a system of government entirely distinct from that which now prevails. I believe that the desire and the motive for large and mighty empires; for gigantic armies and great navies—for those materials which are used for the destruction of life and the desolation of the rewards of labour—will die away; I believe that such things will cease to be necessary, or to be used, when man becomes one family, and freely exchanges the fruits of his labour with his brother man. I believe that, if we could be allowed to reappear on this sublunary scene, we should see, at a far distant period, the governing system of this world revert to something like the municipal system; and I believe that the speculative philosopher of a thousand years hence will date the greatest revolution that ever happened in the world's history from the triumph of the principle which we have met here to advocate. I believe these things: but, whatever may have been my dreams and speculations, I have never obtruded them upon others. I have never acted upon personal or interested motives in this question; I seek no alliance with parties, or favour from parties, and I will take none; but, having the feeling I have of the sacredness of the principle, I say that I can never agree to tamper with it. I, at least, will never be suspected of doing otherwise than pursuing it disinterestedly, honestly, and resolutely. *Manchester Guardian*, 16 January 1846

___

11 Anti-Corn Law League   Bill (*opposite*)

A typical product of the League's presses. Thousands of bills like this appeared all over the country. Wafers for sealing envelopes, tracts, crockery and woodwork bearing anti-Corn Law propaganda, a whole range of propaganda devices were

WORKING MEN!

You Pay a Tax of Tenpence

Upon every Stone of Flour you and your wives and little ones consume.

If there was not the Infamous CORN LAW you and your Families might buy THREE LOAVES for the same money that you now pay for Two.

Upon every Shilling you spend for Bread, Meat, Bacon, Eggs, Vegetables, &c., you pay 4d. Tax for Monopoly.

DOWN, DOWN

WITH THE

Infamous Bread Tax !

GIVE US THIS DAY OUR DAILY BREAD!

NATIONAL ANTI-CORN LAW LEAGUE,

John Johnson — is a Registered Member

Joseph Hickin

Nᵒ 191. Registered by Thos. Wale

issued by the League. Tullie House Museum, Carlisle, possesses an anti-corn law waistcoat, covered with ears of corn. League breadboards carried around their edge the legend 'Give us this day our daily bread', a text much employed by the League.

In addition to these devices the League had more subtle methods, secretly buying press support, and secretly subsidising books and journals—such as *The Economist*—which could be relied on to forward the cause of Free Trade.

---

12 Anti-Corn Law League Membership Card (*opposite*)

Membership card of the National Anti-Corn Law League. This card, in the author's possession, shows a characteristic League line of moralistic and religious argument. There is a view of Bethlehem on the other side.

13 John Waddington Continuation of the Congregational History

One obviously unscrupulous use of the League's capacity for organisation was the conference of ministers of religion which met at Manchester in 1841 to discuss the Corn Laws. The proceedings of this conference were a regular quarry for Free Trade orators, and it was used as a great stroke of propaganda. In 1852 one of the League's apologists, the Rev Henry Dunckley, described this event in the following words: '. . . Amid the impressive rites of devotion, the spirit of monopoly was fearlessly brought to the touchstone of sacred truth, and laden with a Christian's curse. . . .' If, however, we turn to the account given in Waddington's *Continuation of the Congregational History*, it will be obvious that some of those actually participating had their doubts about the proceedings.

. . . It is difficult to pronounce an opinion of the late conference. I viewed the experiment as fearfully hazardous, but I think it has been remarkably preserved from many dangers. I should, however, fear the recurrence of such meetings, although I think the expression of opinion by the ministers of our own denomination perfectly justifiable. Of the late meeting, I should say it cannot be viewed as the expression of our denomination. Yet, still, it was a very important meeting, and had excited amazing interest throughout the manufacturing districts. I felt rather jealous for the *honour of our own body, and did not quite like the multitude of sects with which they were mingled, and the persons of all sorts who called themselves preachers.*

Of the meeting I must say that it was managed with amazing tact, skill, energy, and power. I do not think on any other subject, or in any other place, such a meeting could be obtained. This arose partly from the unbounded liberality of the Anti-Corn-Law League, who furnished clerks, messengers, doorkeepers, assistants of all kinds, printing, feeding, etc., at the will of the secretaries; partly from the power, and energy, and untiring perseverance, of the secretaries and committees . . . there were many of the Manchester ministers, who devoted themselves to preparing measures, and several others who were scarcely ever in the hall, but sitting in the committee rooms from seven in the morning until ten in the evening. Moreover, the thing never came to a *Conference* at all, but only a convocation. There was no discussion. The Committee took care to provide resolutions which were moved and seconded, and then to receive information. The room being crowded with spectators checked discussion, which was I think fortunate. Besides, the feeling was so general in favour of the extreme view—no "protection", no "fixed duty"—that no person on the other side would have any chance. As an effort of generalship, nothing could have been more complete. . . . John Waddington. *Continuation of the Congregational History*, pp 557 et seq, London, 1878

14 Cobden/Henry Cole   Cobden Papers

Other sides of the League's propaganda machine were equally unscrupulous. The humanitarian campaign for improvement in factory conditions which Lord Ashley (the later Lord Shaftesbury) was leading was unwelcome to most of the

Leaguers, and even Cobden was capable of vitriolic attacks on Ashley, as the following two excerpts from his letters show.

The Landowner and the Factory Child.

This is my idea for the Factory Child and Lord Ashley. A tall mill & high chimney in back—clock at 5 a.m. Two or three pale & starved children going to work with large bits of bread in their hands. Lord Ashley has taken the bread from the first child & has broken it in two, & whilst putting the larger share in his pocket & returning the smaller to the child, he lifts up his eyes & in a very sanctimonious tone says "I will never rest until the poor factory child is protected by a ten hours bill from the tyranny of the *merciless & griping millowners*". This last is a quotation from Lord Ashley. There should be a good likeness. . . . Cobden/Henry Cole. *Cobden Papers*, 12 June 1839.

. . . If Mr. Thackeray's next effort should be "the factory children and their protector" I hope he will not fail to secure a good likeness of Lord Ashley. The spice of the cut will be in the resemblance to that aristocratic & canting simpleton; and we shall take care that every member of both houses receives a copy. The Clubs too must be strewn with these things. Cobden/Henry Cole. *Cobden Papers*, 27 June 1839

---

15 Edwin Elliott Poetical Works of Ebenezer Elliott The Northern Star The Corn Laws and Emigration

Verse, too, was called in to fight against the Corn Laws. Ebenezer Elliott, a poet whose acclaim has not lasted, was a prolific versifier in the cause of Free Trade, earning the title of the Corn Law Rhymer.

The second poem comes from the Chartist *Northern Star*. Although most Chartists disliked the Corn Laws, they usually disliked the predominantly middle-class and manufacturing League much more. Here, however, is one illustration of anti-Corn Law feeling from the most notable Chartist newspaper.

(i) *The Corn Law Rhymer*

SONG.

Tune—"*Robin Adair.*"

CHILD, is thy father dead?
  Father is gone!
Why did they tax his bread?
  God's will be done!
Mother has sold her bed;
Better to die than wed!
Where shall she lay her head?
  Home we have none!

Father clamm'd thrice a week—
  God's will be done!
Long for work did he seek,
  Work he found none.
Tears on his hollow cheek
Told what no tongue could speak:
Why did his master break?
  God's will be done!

Doctor said air was best—
  Food we had none;
Father, with panting breast,
  Groan'd to be gone:
Now he is with the blest—
Mother says death is best!
We have no place of rest—
  Yes, ye have one!

Poetical Works of Ebenezer Elliott, edited by his son Edwin, p 381,
London, 1876

(ii) *A Chartist attack on the Corn Laws*

THE CORN LAWS AND EMIGRATION

BECAUSE our lords have taxed the staff of life,
The working man, his children, and his wife
All slave together, yet they must not eat—
Toil gives an appetite, but brings no meat!
The price of bread by law is kept so high,
That what we earn suffices not to buy.
But, why is this? what makes our bread so dear?
Far cheaper 'tis abroad than it is here!
Yes, but a tax is laid on foreign grain,
To make our home-grown corn its price maintain;
And half-fed men may toil, and starve, and die,
That idle lords may lift their heads on high.

We might buy cheap, but landlords want great rents,
To spend in keeping grand establishments.
Their feasts, their fancies, jewels, balls, and plays,
The poor man's nakedness and hunger pays.
The tenant says, if corn comes duty free,
'Twill bring down prices here, and ruin me:
Taxes and rents in England are so high,
I cannot sell so cheap as you could buy.
Pensions, and perquisites, all other prices
Must come down too, save luxuries and vices.
The honest husbandman must emigrate,
And leave poor peasants to increase the rate,
Unless our lords consent to live on less,
And pride succumb to humble happiness!

The Northern Star, 1 January 1842

_____

16 Sir Robert Peel   Speech in Parliament

Only the major political parties could repeal the Corn Laws,
since such a step required legislation. In 1841 Peel won a major

F

general election victory, and in the ensuing years used his strong position to liberalise trade. In his first great budget of 1842 he modified the 1828 Corn Laws, with a new sliding scale set at lower levels. He also reimposed a direct income tax, avowedly as a temporary measure, and reduced import duties on a whole variety of articles. In 1843 a further breach in protection came with the Canada Corn Act, part of a bargain intended to allow Canadian corn easy entrance into the home market and to keep Canada economically independent of the USA. None of these measures seemed to cause any disaster to British agriculture, and trade instead showed much improvement from the depression of 1837–42. Encouraged by this, Peel determined to try the same methods again. In 1845 he reimposed the income tax for a further period, using its revenue to replace that lost by further cuts in import duties. This long quotation from the speech in which he brought forward his 1845 proposals shows the way in which Peel was moving, and the arguments which caused him to reduce the remaining protective tariffs.

I know it does not conduce to popularity to make a proposition for increased or for continued taxation; but it is the duty of a Government to consider the prospects of the future, as well as the present exigencies of the country, and if they are satisfied that the public interest demands a continuance of taxation, even though it may be unpopular, it becomes their duty respectfully to submit to this House the consideration of a proposal on that important subject. We are convinced that it is our duty to propose a continuance of the Property Tax for a further period; and before I am led to ask the assent of this House, or any Gentleman in this House, to that proposal, I feel it is absolutely necessary that I should explain, as I shall now proceed to do, what are the views of Her Majesty's Government with respect to the appropriation of the surplus revenue which will be placed at their disposal after fully providing for every exigency of the Public Service. I know well, as the noble Lord opposite stated the other night, that it is impossible to give an opinion upon the question, abstractedly, can the Property Tax be continued or not? without knowing what are the measures in respect of relief from taxation which would follow as a consequence of its continued imposition. Let me assume for the present—and I merely assume it for the purpose of argument and to make my statement more clear—let me assume, I repeat, for the present, that the House has granted the continuance of the Property Tax. I will then give a short estimate of the revenue arising from it, together with other sources. Suppose, then, the Property Tax to be continued, the estimate of the Revenue for the next year, on the 5th of April, 1846, aided by the 5,200,000*l.* of the Property Tax for the whole year, would be 53,700,000*l.*; and as long as the other sources of the revenue remain equally productive, and as long as the Property Tax is continued, 53,700,000*l.*, subject to a reduction of 600,000*l.*, will be the amount of the Revenue. This 600,000*l.* is the amount received as China money; it will be continued next year; but as that is merely a temporary addition, I think it is better, for the purpose of calculating the Revenue to strike it out altogether. The Revenue for the year, then, on the 5th of April, 1846, assuming the Property Tax to be continued, deducting this sum of 600,000*l.*, will be 53,100,000*l.* The charge for the debt, and on account of the different branches of the public service, will be 49,690,000*l.*; so that there will be left, on the 5th of April, 1846, and in successive years as long as the Income Tax continues, and the other sources of the revenue remain equally productive, a net surplus of 3,409,000*l.* That is the surplus that will remain if the House should acquiesce in the proposal which I shall make to increase the expenditure on the Navy, and shall also determine that the Income Tax shall be continued. I now, Sir, approach that most important part of my statement I have this night to make, namely, what is the mode in which that surplus, or any part of that surplus, shall be applied for the relief of taxation. What are the inducements, apart from that of providing effectually for the public service, which I can hold out to the House of Commons as a motive to obtain their consent to the continuance of the Income Tax? I should not have proposed to the House the continuance of the Income Tax unless I had the strongest persuasion, partly founded on the experience of the last three years, that it will be competent to the House of Commons, by continuing the Income Tax, to make such arrangements with respect to general taxation as shall be the foundation of great commercial prosperity, and shall materially add to the comforts even of those who are called on to contribute to the Income Tax. When the question is, having a considerable surplus, to determine how that surplus can be most efficiently employed, the subject becomes worthy of the most important and serious consideration. In the first place you have to consider the claims which may be urged in favour of a reduction of taxation on account of the heaviness with which certain imposts press on articles of general consumption. You are bound also to consider what taxes press on the raw materials which constitute the staple of the manufactures of the country. You are also bound to consider what taxes cause a great increase in the establishments necessary for their collection, and what are those taxes the remission of which will enable us to diminish those establishments, so as to reduce the expense of collection. We are bound also to consider what are those taxes, the removal of which will give more scope to commercial enterprise, and occasion an increased demand for labour. I will not say which of these considerations ought to be the most predominant—all ought to occupy our serious attention, for all are of the very greatest importance. If we receive the sanction of the House for the continuance of the Income Tax, we shall feel it to be our duty to make a great experiment with respect to taxation, and we shall hope that the general prosperity which will result therefrom will contribute to fill up the void caused by the cessation of the Income Tax in future years. We do not propose to maintain any material surplus of revenue over expenditure, confident that, whatever may happen, this House is determined to maintain the public credit. We have determined to recommend extensive reductions in those taxes which, in our opinion, press more onerously on the community than the Income Tax. . . . Remember this—and I do not conceal the fact, for it ought to enter into your consideration when deciding the question, whether you will continue the Income Tax—that during its operation the Revenue has so prospered that the receipts at present, independently of the Income Tax, are almost equal to the national expenditure. Such has been the increase of revenue from permanent sources of income during the existence of the Income Tax, that we might have avoided making this experiment; we might have provided for the supplies of the present year without making any application to Parliament in respect to increased taxation; but we propose to continue the Income Tax for a further period, not for the purpose of providing the Supplies for the year, but distinctly for the purpose of enabling us to make this great experiment of reducing other taxes. The term for which I suggest the continuance of it will not exceed that for which it was originally imposed. I cannot say, when urging these extensive reductions—I will not say that it might not have been a wiser course to give a longer period to test the efficacy of the plan; but at the same time it is natural that Parliament should ask to have the control of the tax at a period not more remote than that for which it was in the first instance enacted. Therefore I do not propose that it should be renewed for more than three years, and I hope the House will not insist upon a shorter period. It would be impossible to enter upon these extensive reductions of taxation, unless we had the assurance that this great source of revenue would not be dried up at least during the next three years; and at the expiration of three years it is my confident belief that that will have again occurred which has now occurred, and that it will be competent to Parliament then to dispense, as it might now, with the Income Tax. I have that reliance upon the elasticity of the resources of this Empire, that I do expect, before the termination of three years, that this repeal of taxes will have produced beneficial effects, and that we shall find an increase of revenue probably enabling us to dispense with the continuance of the Income Tax. But let the House remember that the principle on which we have gone, and gone advisedly, is the absolute repeal of taxation in many cases; we do not diminish a tax, on glass for instance, keeping on one-quarter or one-half of it; we do not lower the duty on auctions, on cotton wool, or on articles of smaller imputation: but we propose the absolute repeal, expecting from the increased consumption of other taxed articles, an equivalent improvement in the Revenue. We do hope that the direct and instant effect will be increased consumption of many articles now subject to duty, invigorating the industry and extending the commercial enterprise of the country through other channels, and supplying the void we cannot hope to fill up by direct taxation. Sir, I believe I have now executed the task I proposed to myself. I have, however imperfectly, explained the views and intentions of Her Majesty's Government with respect to the financial and commercial policy of the country. I trust that the House will now, as it did on the former occasion, without pronouncing a hasty or a precipitate judgment, take into its consideration comprehensively the whole of the plan. I hope it will reflect, whether or no, upon the whole, it be for the interest of the country to adopt it; and, after mature deliberation, I confidently believe that the decision of the House will be in its favour. Whatever may be the decision, at any rate, we have the consolation of knowing that we have not sought popularity by avoiding the question of continuing the Property Tax: we have not acted in deference to popular clamour, for we have selected taxes for reduction and abolition against which there has been no agitation. I know it will be said that the principles I have laid down are capable of much further extension, and that in deference to them I ought to have made much greater reductions in Import Duties; but it is our object, while we establish good principles, to allow for the present state of society, and viewing the magnitude of the interests involved, the consequence to those interests of rash and hasty interference, it is our desire to realise the utmost degree of good, without disturbance or alarm to interests which cannot be disturbed or alarmed without paralysing industry. Sir, I submit, this proposal on behalf of Her Majesty's Government to the judgment of the House. We have taken this course after careful consideration, and we recommend this plan from a deliberate conviction that if sanctioned by Parliament it will conduce to the extension of industry, to the encouragement of enterprise, and that the result of that extension of industry and encouragement of enterprise will be the benefit of all classes of the community, whether they are directly or indirectly connected with commerce, manufactures, or agriculture. Our conviction is, that by the adoption of this proposal, industry and commerce will be immediately benefited, and that indirectly all classes of this vast community will find its welfare promoted. Hansard's *Parliamentary Debates*, 3rd Series, Vol LXXVII, cols 471–3, 495–7, 14 February 1845

17 Lord John Russell   Letter to his Constituents

The other major political group was moving in the same direction as Peel. In 1841 the Whig government of Lord Melbourne, then facing its final defeat, had determined to replace the sliding scale of the 1828 Corn Law with a moderate fixed import duty on foreign food. Their expulsion from office prevented this, and in the next few years their policy on commercial matters, in so far as they had one, favoured even lower duties. Then, in 1845, the Irish potato famine helped to resolve their difficulties. In a letter written from Edinburgh to his London constituents in November, Lord John Russell, the Whig leader, declared in favour of repealing the Corn Laws. Now, for the first time, a potential government was ready to adopt the policy of the League.

To the Electors of the City of London.

Gentlemen,—The present state of the country, in regard to its supply of food, cannot be viewed without apprehension. Forethought and bold precaution may avert any serious evils; indecision and procrastination may produce a state of suffering which it is frightful to contemplate.

Three weeks ago it was generally expected that Parliament

would be immediately called together. The announcement that Ministers were prepared at that time to advise the Crown to summon Parliament, and to propose on their first meeting a suspension of the import duties on corn, would have caused orders at once to be sent to various ports of Europe and America for the purchase and transmission of grain for the consumption of the United Kingdom. An Order in Council dispensing with the law was neither necessary nor desirable. No party in Parliament would have made itself responsible for the obstruction of a measure so urgent and so beneficial.

The Queen's Ministers have met, and separated, without affording us any promise of such seasonable relief.

It becomes us, therefore, the Queen's subjects, to consider how we can best avert, or at all events mitigate, calamities of no ordinary magnitude.

Two evils require your consideration. One of these is the disease in the potatoes, affecting very seriously parts of England and Scotland, and committing fearful ravages in Ireland.

The extent of this evil has not yet been ascertained, and every week, indeed, tends either to reveal unexpected disease, or to abate in some districts the alarm previously entertained. But there is one misfortune peculiar to the failure in this particular crop. The effect of a bad corn harvest is, in the first place, to diminish the supply in the market, and to raise the price. Hence diminished consumption, and the privation of incipient scarcity, by which the whole stock is more equally distributed over the year, and the ultimate pressure is greatly mitigated. But the fear of the breaking out of this unknown disease in the potatoes induces the holders to hurry into the market, and thus we have at one and the same time rapid consumption and impending deficiency—scarcity of the article and cheapness of price. The ultimate suffering must thereby be rendered far more severe than it otherwise would be. The evil to which I have adverted may be owing to an adverse season, to a mysterious disease in the potato, to want of science or of care in propagating the plant. In any of these cases Government is no more subject to blame for the failure of the potato crop than it was entitled to credit for the plentiful corn harvests which we have lately enjoyed.

Another evil, however, under which we are suffering, is the fruit of Ministerial counsel and Parliamentary law. It is the direct consequence of an Act of Parliament, passed three years ago, on the recommendation of the present advisers of the Crown. By this law grain of all kinds has been made subject to very high duties on importation. These duties are so contrived that the worse the quality of the corn the higher is the duty; so that when good wheat rises to 70s. a quarter, the average price of all wheat is 57s. or 58s., and the duty 15s. or 14s. a quarter. Thus the corn barometer points to fair, while the ship is bending under a storm.

This defect was pointed out many years ago by writers on the corn laws, and was urged upon the attention of the House of Commons when the present Act was under consideration.

But I confess that on the general subject my views have in the course of twenty years undergone a great alteration. I used to be of opinion that corn was an exception to the general rules of political economy; but observation and experience have convinced me that we ought to abstain from all interference with the supply of food. Neither a government nor a legislature can ever regulate the corn market with the beneficial effects which the entire freedom of sale and purchase are sure of themselves to produce.

I have for several years endeavoured to obtain a compromise on this subject. In 1839 I voted for a committee of the whole House, with the view of supporting the substitution of a moderate fixed duty for the sliding scale. In 1841 I announced the intention of the then Government of proposing a fixed duty of 8s. a quarter. In the past session I proposed the imposition of some lower duty. These propositions were successively rejected. The present First Lord of the Treasury met them in 1839, 1840, and 1841 by eloquent panegyrics of the existing system—the plenty it had caused, the rural happiness it had diffused. He met the proposition for diminished protection in the same way in which he had met the offer of securities for Protestant interests in 1817 and

1825—in the same way in which he met the proposal to allow Manchester, Leeds, and Birmingham to send members to Parliament in 1830.

The result of resistance to qualified concessions must be the same in the present instance as in those I have mentioned. It is no longer worth while to contend for a fixed duty. In 1841 the Free Trade party would have agreed to a duty of 8s. a quarter on wheat, and after a lapse of years this duty might have been further reduced, and ultimately abolished. But the imposition of any duty at present, without a provision for its extinction within a short period, would but prolong a contest already sufficiently fruitful of animosity and discontent. The struggle to make bread scarce and dear, when it is clear that part, at least, of the additional price goes to increase rent, is a struggle deeply injurious to an aristocracy which (this quarrel once removed) is strong in property, strong in the construction of our legislature, strong in opinion, strong in ancient associations, and the memory of immortal services.

Let us, then, unite to put an end to a system which has been proved to be the blight of commerce, the bane of agriculture, the source of bitter divisions among classes, the cause of penury, fever, mortality, and crime among the people.

But if this end is to be achieved, it must be gained by the unequivocal expression of the public voice. It is not to be denied that many elections for cities and towns in 1841, and some in 1845, appear to favour the assertion that Free Trade is not popular with the great mass of the community. The Government appear to be waiting for some excuse to give up the present corn law. Let the people, by petition, by address, by remonstrance, afford them the excuse they seek. Let the Ministry propose such a revision of the taxes as in their opinion may render the public burdens more just and more equal; let them add any other provisions which caution and even scrupulous forbearance may suggest; but let the removal of restrictions on the admission of the main articles of food and clothing used by the mass of the people be required, in plain terms, as useful to all great interests, and indispensable to the progress of the nation.—I have the honour to be, Gentlemen, your obedient servant,

J. RUSSELL.

Edinburgh: November 22, 1845.

Spencer Walpole. *Life of Lord John Russell*, Vol I, pp 406–9, London, 1889

___

18 Sir Robert Peel   Speech in Parliament

Peel struck the final blow against the Corn Laws in 1846. As a result his Conservative party split, and a factious alliance between the Whig opposition and the protectionists drove him from office by combining to defeat the government's proposals to strengthen the forces of law and order in a famine-stricken Ireland.

The last two paragraphs of this excerpt again show how Free Trade was not considered just an economic theory, but a cause with strong overtones of sentiment and romanticism. This passage is taken from the resignation speech delivered by Peel to the House of Commons on 29 June 1846.

___

Sir, I have reason to believe that the noble Lord the Member for the city of London has been commanded by the Queen to repair to Her Majesty for the purpose of rendering his assistance in the formation of a Government. I presume the general principle upon which the Government to be formed by the noble Lord will act, so far as its commercial policy is concerned, will be the continued application of those principles which tend to establish a freer intercourse with other countries. If that policy be pursued, as I confidently expect it will, I shall feel it to be my duty to give to the Government, in the furtherance of it, my cordial support. If other countries choose to buy in the dearest market, such an option on their part constitutes no reason why we should not be permitted to buy in the cheapest. I trust the Government of the noble Lord will not resume the policy which they and we have felt most inconvenient, namely, the haggling with foreign countries about reciprocal concessions, instead of taking that independent course which we believe to be conducive to our own interests. Let us trust to the influence of public opinion in other countries—let us trust that our example, with the proof of practical benefit we derive from it, will at no remote period insure the adoption of the principles on which we have acted, rather than defer indefinitely that which *per se* is advantageous to ourselves, in the hope of obtaining by delay equivalent concessions from other countries. Sir, when I express the confident hope that these general principles will influence the commercial policy of the new Government, I do not advise that the adoption of them should overrule every moral consideration, or should at once subject every species of production in this country to competition with other nations. I speak generally as to the tendency of our commercial policy. I trust that every step that is taken will be towards the relaxation of restriction upon trade. I, for one, shall not urge upon the Government a hasty and precipitate adoption of principles sound in themselves, if through the abrupt and sudden application of them, we incur the risk of a great derangement of the social system. I shall bear in mind that vast experiments have been recently made under the present Administration—I shall bear in mind also, that the surplus amount of public revenue is smaller than it ought to be, consistently with the permanent interests of the country. While, therefore, I offer a cordial support in enforcing those general principles of commercial policy which have received the sanction of Parliament in the present Session, I shall not urge the Government to any such simultaneous and precipitate extension of them as may be either injurious to interests entitled from special circumstances to some degree of continued protection, or may incur the risk of deranging the financial system of the country. In delivering these opinions, I am bound to say that I am rather indicating my own intentions and the course I shall individually pursue, than that I have had the opportunity of conferring with others, and am authorized to speak their sentiments. I cannot doubt, however, that those who gave their cordial concurrence to the commercial measures which I have proposed, will be ready to give their general acquiescence and support to measures of a similar character when proposed by others. . . . In relinquishing power, I shall leave a name, severely censured I fear by many who, on public grounds, deeply regret the severance of party ties—deeply regret that severance, not from interested or personal motives, but from the firm conviction that fidelity to party engagements—the existence and maintenance of a great party—constitutes a powerful instrument of government: I shall surrender power severely censured also, by others who, from no interested motive, adhere to the principle of protection, considering the maintenance of it to be essential to the welfare and interests of the country: I shall leave a name execrated by every monopolist who, from less honourable motives, clamours for protection because it conduces to his own individual benefit; but it may be that I shall leave a name sometimes remembered with expressions of good will in the abodes of those whose lot it is to labour, and to earn their daily bread by the sweat of their brow, when they shall recruit their exhausted strength with abundant and untaxed food, the sweeter because it is no longer leavened by a sense of injustice. *Parliamentary Debates*, Third Series, Vol LXXXVII, 1047–55, 29 June 1846

19 House of Lords   Protest against the Repeal of the Corn Laws

The protectionist peers, unable to prevent the repeal of the Corn Laws, entered a number of formal protests against this measure on the Journals of the House of Lords. This section ends with the first of these, which had the most signatures and was the most fully argued.

The following Protests against the Third Reading of the Bill to Amend the Laws relating to the Importation of Corn were entered on the Journals:—

(No. 1.)

Dissentient—

1. Because the repeal of the Corn Laws will greatly increase

the dependence of this country upon foreign countries for its supply of food, and will thereby expose it to dangers against which former statesmen have thought it essential to take legislative precautions.

2. Because there is no security nor probability that other nations will take similar steps; and this country will, therefore, not only be exposed to the risks of failure of supply consequent on a state of war, but will also be exclusively subject to an unlimited influx of corn in times of abundance, and to sudden checks whenever short crops shall reduce the ordinary supply from the exporting countries, or their Governments shall deem it necessary to take precautionary measures for their own protection, thus causing rapid and disastrous fluctuations in the markets of this country.

3. Because under a system of protection the agriculture of this country has more than kept pace with the increasing demand of its increasing population; and because it is to be apprehended that the removal of protection may throw some lands out of cultivation, and check in others the progress of improvement which has led to this satisfactory result.

4. Because it is unjust to withdraw protection from the landed interest of this country, while that interest remains subject to exclusive burdens imposed for purposes of general, and not of special advantage.

5. Because the loss to be sustained by the repeal of the Corn Laws will fall most heavily on the least wealthy portion of the landed proprietors, will press immediately and severely on the tenant-farmers, and through them, with ruinous consequences, on the agricultural labourers.

6. Because indirectly, but not less certainly, injurious consequences will result to the manufacturing interest, and especially to the artisans and mechanics, from competition with the agricultural labourers thrown out of employment, but principally from the loss of the home market, caused by the inability of the producers of grain, and those dependent on them, to consume manufactured goods to the same extent as heretofore.

7. Because the same cause will produce similar evil results to the tradesmen, retail dealers, and others in country towns, not themselves engaged in agricultural pursuits, but mainly dependent for their subsistence on their dealings with those who are so engaged.

8. Because the effect of a repeal of the Corn Laws will be especially injurious to Ireland, by lowering the value of her principal exports, and by still further reducing the demand for labour, the want of which is among the principal evils of her social condition.

9. Because a free trade in corn will cause a large and unnecessary diminution of annual income, thus impairing the revenue of the country, at the same time that it cripples the resources of those classes on whom the weight of local taxation now mainly falls.

10. Because a general reduction of prices, consequent on reduction of the price of corn, will tend unduly to raise the monied interest at the expense of all others, and to aggravate the pressure of the national burdens.

11. Because the removal of differential duties in favour of Canadian corn is at variance with the legislative encouragement held out to that Colony by Parliament, on the faith of which the colonists have laid out large sums upon the improvement of their internal navigation; and because the removal of protection will divert the traffic of the interior from the St. Lawrence and the British ports of Montreal and Quebec, to the foreign port of New York; thus throwing out of employment a large amount of British shipping, severing the commercial interests of Canada from those of the parent country, and connecting those interests most intimately with the United States of America.

12. Because the adoption of a similar system with regard to other articles of commerce will tend to sever the strongest bond of union between this country and her Colonies, will deprive the British merchant of that which is now his most certain market, and sap the foundation of that colonial system, to which, com-

mercially and politically, this country owes much of its present greatness.

STANLEY	ASHBURTON
RICHMOND	GAGE
EXETER	CADOGAN
HARDWICKE	NORTHWICK
WARWICK	H. EXETER
MALMESBURY	BUCKINGHAM AND CHANDOS
LUCAN	DELAWARR
STANHOPE	CANTERBURY
G. ROCHESTER	CLEVELAND
FEVERSHAM	C. BANGOR
BOLTON	MANVERS
HASTINGS	BERESFORD
DONERAILE	SOMERS
SOUTHAMPTON	TANKERVILLE
SALTOUN	MANSFIELD
PENSHURST	ABINGER
SKELMERSDALE	BEAUMONT
KENYON	ORFORD
BOSTON	LOVELL AND HOLLAND
HAY	SHEFFIELD
NEWCASTLE	AIRLIE
MARLBOROUGH	BEVERLEY
SANDWICH	COLCHESTER
WILTON	POMFRET
REDESDALE	SHERBORNE
RUTLAND	GRAHAM
CARLETON	DIGBY
ST. VINCENT	COMBERMERE
OXFORD AND MORTIMER	COLVILLE OF CULROSS
MUNSTER	SONDES
BEAUFORT	CHESTERFIELD
BERWICK	ARDROSSAN
ELDON	RANFURLY

GASCOIGNE SALISBURY

ORKNEY

GRANTLEY

LOFTUS

H. GLOUCESTER AND BRISTOL

SELKIRK

TEMPLEMORE

CHARLEVILLE

DARTMOUTH

NELSON

STRADBROOKE

POLWARTH

LAKE

WILLOUGHBY D'ERESBY

BRADFORD

VAUX OF HARROWDEN

CARNARVON

BRODRICKE

CROFTON

DE FREYNE

CAWDOR

CLANCARTY

LORTON

Parliamentary Debates, Third Series, Vol LXXXVII, 961–3

G

PART THREE

The Zenith of Free Trade

The repeal of the Corn Laws was followed in the next few years by the final repeal of the Navigation Laws and by the disappearance of remaining protective duties. At first the Conservative opposition fought against the further encroachments of Free Trade, but, after the general election of 1852 reaffirmed the decision of 1846, Derby and Disraeli realised that protection was dead for the time being at least. Free Trade remained dominant in economic theory, as can be seen from a relevant passage in John Stuart Mill's *Principles of Political Economy* (20). G. R. Porter, whom we have already met in connection with the 1840 Import Duties Committee, was another prominent writer who supported Free Trade (21).

The victorious Free Traders were quick to hail the success of their cause, and to hymn the advantages and significance of their triumph (22). After 1852 all important political groups supported Free Trade, and Gladstone was one of its most fervent devotees (23).

Although for thirty years after 1846 Free Trade was clearly in the ascendant, there were from time to time mutterings of doubt. The Christian Socialists, led by men like F. D. Maurice (1805–72) and the novelist Charles Kingsley (1819–75), disliked what seemed to them the socially irresponsible and materialistic elements in the doctrines of the Manchester School of Cobden and Bright (24). This group, however, though it contained a number of able and energetic men, had little practical influence. The third quarter of the nineteenth century was the heyday of Free Trade in Britain.

20 John Stuart Mill   Principles of Political Economy

The *Principles of Political Economy* by John Stuart Mill (1806–73), was first published in 1848. The following passage is taken from Chapter X, 'Of Interference of Government Grounded on Erroneous Theories'.

J. S. Mill was one of the most influential writers of the century on economics and political theory.

---

§ 1. [*Doctrine of Protection to Native Industry*] From the necessary functions of government, and the effects produced on the economical interests of society by their good or ill discharge, we proceed to the functions which belong to what I have termed, for want of a better designation, the optional class; those which are sometimes assumed by governments and sometimes not, and which it is not unanimously admitted that they ought to exercise.

Before entering on the general principles of the question, it will be advisable to clear from our path all those cases, in which government interference works ill because grounded on false views of the subject interfered with. Such cases have no connexion with any theory respecting the proper limits of interference. There are some things with which governments ought not to meddle, and other things with which they ought; but whether right or wrong in itself, the interference must work for ill, if government, not understanding the subject which it meddles with, meddles to bring about a result which would be mischievous. We will therefore begin by passing in review various false theories, which have from time to time formed the ground of acts of government more or less economically injurious.

Former writers on political economy have found it needful to devote much trouble and space to this department of their subject. It has now happily become possible, at least in our own country, greatly to abridge this purely negative part of our discussions. The false theories of political economy which have done so much mischief in times past, are entirely discredited among all who have not lagged behind the general progress of opinion; and few of the enactments which were once grounded on those theories still help to deform the statute-book. As the principles on which their condemnation rests have been fully set forth in other parts of this Treatise, we may here content ourselves with a few brief indications.

Of these false theories, the most notable is the doctrine of Protection to Native Industry; a phrase meaning the prohibition, or the discouragement by heavy duties, of such foreign commodities as are capable of being produced at home. If the theory involved in this system had been correct, the practical conclusions grounded on it would not have been unreasonable. The theory was, that to buy things produced at home was a national benefit, and the introduction of foreign commodities generally a national loss. It being at the same time evident that the interest of the consumer is to buy foreign commodities in preference to domestic whenever they are either cheaper or better, the interest of the consumer appeared in this respect to be contrary to the public interest; he was certain, if left to his own inclinations, to do what according to the theory was injurious to the public.

It was shown, however, in our analysis of the effects of international trade, as it had been often shown by former writers, that the importation of foreign commodities, in the common course of traffic, never takes place, except when it is, economically speaking, a national good, by causing the same amount of commodities to be obtained at a smaller cost of labour and capital to the country. To prohibit, therefore, this importation, or impose duties which prevent it, is to render the labour and capital of the country less efficient in production than they would otherwise be; and compel a waste, of the difference between the labour and capital necessary for the home production of the commodity, and that which is required for producing the things with which it can be purchased from abroad. The amount of national loss thus occasioned is measured by the excess of the price at which the commodity is produced over that at which it could be imported. In the case of manufactured goods, the whole difference between the two prices is absorbed in indemnifying the producers for waste of labour, or of the capital which supports that labour. Those who are supposed to be benefited, namely, the makers of the protected articles, (unless they form an exclusive company, and have a monopoly against their own countrymen as well as against foreigners,) do not obtain higher profits than other people. All is sheer loss, to the country as well as to the consumer. When the protected article is a product of agriculture —the waste of labour not being incurred on the whole produce, but only on what may be called the last instalment of it—the extra price is only in part an indemnity for waste, the remainder being a tax paid to the landlords.

The restrictive and prohibitory policy was originally grounded on what is called the Mercantile System, which representing the advantage of foreign trade to consist solely in bringing money into the country, gave artificial encouragement to exportation of goods, and discountenanced their importation. The only exceptions to the system were those required by the system itself. The materials and instruments of production were the subjects of a contrary policy, directed however to the same end; they were freely imported, and not permitted to be exported, in order that manufacturers, being more cheaply supplied with the requisites of manufacture, might be able to sell cheaper, and therefore to export more largely. For a similar reason, importation was allowed and even favoured, when confined to the productions of countries which were supposed to take from the country still more than it took from them, thus enriching it by a favourable balance of trade. As part of the same system, colonies were founded, for the supposed advantage of compelling them to buy our commodities, or at all events not to buy those of any other country: in return for which restriction, we were generally willing to come under an equivalent obligation with respect to the staple productions of the colonists. The consequences of the theory were pushed so far, that it was not unusual even to give bounties on exportation, and induce foreigners to buy from us rather than from other countries, by a cheapness which we artificially produced, by paying part of the price for them out of our own taxes. This is a stretch beyond the point yet reached by any private tradesman in his competition for business. No shopkeeper, I should think, ever made a practice of bribing customers by selling goods to them at a permanent loss, making it up to himself from other funds in his possession.

The principle of the Mercantile Theory is now given up even by writers and governments who still cling to the restrictive system. Whatever hold that system has over men's minds, independently of the private interests exposed to real or apprehended loss by its abandonment, is derived from fallacies other than the old notion of the benefits of heaping up money in the country. The most effective of these is the specious plea of employing our own countrymen and our national industry, instead of feeding and supporting the industry of foreigners. The answer to this, from the principles laid down in former chapters, is evident. Without reverting to the fundamental theorem discussed in an early part of the present treatise, respecting the nature and sources of employment for labour, it is sufficient to say, what has usually been said by the advocates of free trade, that the alternative is not between employing our own people and foreigners, but between employing one class and another of our own people. The imported commodity is always paid for, directly or indirectly, with the produce of our own industry: that industry being, at the same time rendered more productive, since, with the same labour and outlay, we are enabled to possess ourselves of a greater quantity of the article. Those who have not well considered the subject are apt to suppose that our exporting an equivalent in our own produce, for the foreign articles we consume, depends on contingencies—on the consent of foreign countries to make some corresponding relaxation of their own restrictions, or on the question whether those from whom we buy are induced by that circumstance to buy more from us; and that, if these things, or things equivalent to them, do not happen, the payment must be made in money. Now, in the first place, there is nothing more objectionable in a money payment than in payment by any other medium, if the state of the market makes it the most advantageous remittance; and the money itself was first acquired, and would again be replenished, by the export of an equivalent value of our own products. But, in the next place, a very short interval of paying in money would so lower prices as either to stop a part of the importation, or raise up a foreign demand for our produce, sufficient to pay for the imports. I grant that this disturbance of the equation of international demand would be in some degree to our disadvantage, in the purchase of other imported articles; and that a country which prohibits some foreign commodities, does, *cæteris paribus*, obtain those which it does not prohibit, at a less price than it would otherwise have to pay. To express the same thing in other words; a country which destroys or prevents altogether certain branches of foreign trade, thereby annihilating a general gain to the world, which would be shared in some proportion between itself and other countries—does, in some circumstances, draw to itself, at the expense of foreigners, a larger share than would else belong to it of the gain arising from that portion of its foreign trade which it suffers to subsist. But even this it can only be enabled to do, if foreigners do not maintain equivalent prohibitions or restrictions against its commodities. In any case, the justice or expediency of destroying one of two gains, in order to engross a rather larger share of the other, does not require much discussion: the gain, too, which is destroyed, being, in proportion to the magnitude of the transactions, the larger of the two, since it is the one which capital, left to itself, is supposed to seek by preference.

Defeated as a general theory, the Protectionist doctrine finds support in some particular cases, from considerations which, when really in point, involve greater interests than mere saving of labour; the interests of national subsistence and of national defence. The discussions on the Corn Laws have familiarized everybody with the plea, that we ought to be independent of foreigners for the food of the people; and the Navigation Laws were grounded, in theory and profession, on the necessity of keeping up a "nursery of seamen" for the navy. On this last subject I at once admit, that the object is worth the sacrifice; and that a country exposed to invasion by sea, if it cannot otherwise have sufficient ships and sailors of its own to secure the means of manning on an emergency an adequate fleet, is quite right in obtaining those means, even at an economical sacrifice in point of cheapness of transport. When the English Navigation Laws were enacted, the Dutch, from their maritime skill and their low rate of profit at home, were able to carry for other nations, England included, at cheaper rates than those nations could carry for themselves: which placed all other countries at a great comparative disadvantage in obtaining experienced seamen for their ships of war. The Navigation Laws, by which this deficiency was remedied, and at the same time a blow struck against the maritime power of a nation with which England was then frequently engaged in hostilities, were probably, though economically disadvantageous, politically expedient. But English ships and sailors can now navigate as cheaply as those of any other country; maintaining at least an equal competition with the other maritime nations even in their own trade. The ends which may once have justified Navigation Laws, require them no longer, and afforded no reason for maintaining this invidious exception to the general rule of free trade.

With regard to subsistence, the plea of the Protectionists has been so often and so triumphantly met, that it requires little notice here. That country is the most steadily as well as the most abundantly supplied with food, which draws its supplies from the largest surface. It is ridiculous to found a general system of policy on so improbable a danger as that of being at war with all the nations of the world at once; or to suppose that, even if inferior at sea, a whole country could be blockaded like a town, or that the growers of food in other countries would not be as anxious not to lose an advantageous market, as we should be not to be deprived of their corn. On the subject, however, of subsistence, there is one point which deserves more especial consideration. In cases of actual or apprehended scarcity, many countries of Europe are accustomed to stop the exportation of food. Is this, or not, sound policy? There can be no doubt that in the present state of international morality, a people cannot, any more than an individual, be blamed for not starving itself to feed others. But if the greatest amount of good to mankind on the whole, were the end aimed at in the maxims of international conduct, such collective churlishness would certainly be condemned by them. Suppose that in ordinary circumstances the trade in food were perfectly free, so that the price in one country could not habitually exceed that in any other by more than the cost of carriage, together with a moderate profit to the importer. A general scarcity ensues, affecting all countries, but in unequal degrees. If the price rose in one country more than in others, it would be a proof that in that country the scarcity was severest, and that by permitting food to go freely thither from any other country, it would be spared from a less urgent necessity to relieve a greater. When the interests, therefore, of all countries are considered, free exportation is desirable. To the exporting country considered separately, it may, at least on the particular occasion, be an inconvenience: but taking into account that the country which is now the giver, will in some future season be the receiver, and the one that is benefited by the freedom, I cannot but think that even to the apprehension of food rioters it might be made apparent, that in such cases they should do to others what they would wish done to themselves.

In countries in which the Protection theory is declining, but not yet given up, such as the United States, a doctrine has come into notice which is a sort of compromise between free trade and restriction, namely, that protection for protection's sake is improper, but that there is nothing objectionable in having as much protection as may incidentally result from a tariff framed solely for revenue. Even in England, regret is sometimes expressed that a "moderate fixed duty" was not preserved on corn, on account of the revenue it would yield. Independently, however, of the general impolicy of taxes on the necessaries of life, this doctrine overlooks the fact, that revenue is received only on the quantity imported, but that the tax is paid on the entire quantity consumed. To make the public pay much that the treasury may receive a little, is not an eligible mode of obtaining a revenue. In the case of manufactured articles the doctrine involves a palpable inconsistency. The object of the duty as a means of revenue, is inconsistent with its affording, even incidentally, any protection. It can only operate as protection in so far as it prevents importation; and to whatever degree it prevents importation, it affords no revenue.

The only case in which, on mere principles of political economy, protecting duties can be defensible, is when they are imposed temporarily (especially in a young and rising nation) in hopes of naturalizing a foreign industry, in itself perfectly suitable to the circumstances of the country. The superiority of one country over another in a branch of production, often arises only from having begun it sooner. There may be no inherent advantage on one part, or disadvantage on the other, but only a present superiority of acquired skill and experience. A country which has this skill and experience yet to acquire, may in other respects be better adapted to the production than those which were earlier in the field: and besides, it is a just remark of Mr. Rae, that nothing has a greater tendency to promote improvements in any branch of production, than its trial under a new set of conditions. But it cannot be expected that individuals should, at their own risk, or rather to their certain loss, introduce a new manufacture, and bear the burthen of carrying it on until the producers have been educated up to the level of those with whom the processes are traditional. A protecting duty, continued for a reasonable time, might sometimes be the least inconvenient mode in which the nation can tax itself for the support of such an experiment. But it is essential that the protection should be confined to cases in which there is good ground of assurance that the industry which it fosters will after a time be able to dispense with it; nor should the domestic producers ever be allowed to expect that it will be continued to them beyond the time necessary for a fair trial of what they are capable of accomplishing.

The only writer, of any reputation as a political economist, who now adheres to the Protectionist doctrine, Mr. H. C. Carey, rests its defence, in an economic point of view, principally on two reasons. One is, the great saving in cost of carriage, consequent on producing commodities at or very near to the place where they are to be consumed. The whole of the cost of carriage, both on the commodities imported and on those exported in exchange for them, he regards as a direct burthen on the producers, and not, as is obviously the truth, on the consumers. On whomsoever it falls, it is, without doubt, a burthen on the industry of the world. But it is obvious (and that Mr. Carey does not see it, is one of the many surprising things in his book) that the burthen is only borne for a more than equivalent advantage. If the commodity is bought in a foreign country with domestic produce in spite of the double cost of carriage, the fact proves that, heavy as that cost may be, the saving in cost of production outweighs it, and the collective labour of the country is on the whole better remunerated than if the article were produced at home. Cost of carriage is a natural protecting duty, which free trade has no power to abrogate: and unless America gained more by obtaining her manufactures through the medium of her corn and cotton than she loses in cost of carriage, the capital employed in producing corn and cotton in annually increased quantities for the foreign market, would turn to manufactures instead. The natural advantages attending a mode of industry in which there is less cost of carriage to pay, can at most be only a justification for a temporary and merely tentative protection. The expenses of production being always greatest at first, it may happen that the home production, though really the most advantageous, may not become so until after a certain duration of pecuniary loss, which it is not to be expected that private speculators should incur in order that their successors may be benefited by their ruin. I have therefore conceded that in a new country a temporary protecting duty may sometimes be economically defensible; on condition, however, that it be strictly limited in point of time, and provision be made that during the latter part of its existence it be on a gradually decreasing scale. Such temporary protection is of the same nature as a patent, and should be governed by similar conditions.

The remaining argument of Mr. Carey in support of the economic benefits of Protectionism, applies only to countries whose exports consist of agricultural produce. He argues, that by a trade of this description they actually send away their soil: the distant consumers not giving back to the land of the country, as home consumers would do, the fertilizing elements which they abstract from it. This argument deserves attention on account of the physical truth on which it is founded; a truth which has only lately come to be understood, but which is henceforth destined to be a permanent element in the thoughts of statesmen, as it must always have been in the destinies of nations. To the question of Protectionism, however, it is irrelevant. That the immense growth of raw produce in America to be consumed in Europe, is progressively exhausting the soil of the Eastern, and even of the older Western States, and that both are already far less productive than formerly, is credible in itself, even if no one bore witness to it. But what I have already said respecting cost of carriage, is true also of the cost of manuring. Free trade does not compel America to export corn: she would cease to do so if it ceased to be to her advantage. As, then, she would not persist in exporting raw produce and importing manufactures, any longer than the labour she saved by doing so exceeded what the carriage cost her, so when it became necessary for her to replace in the soil the elements of fertility which she had sent away, if the saving in cost of production were more than equivalent to the cost of carriage and of manure together, manure would be imported; and if not, the export of corn would cease. It is evident that one of these two things would already have taken place, if there had not been near at hand a constant succession of new soils, not yet exhausted of their fertility, the cultivation of which enables her, whether judiciously or not, to postpone the question of manure. As soon as it no longer answers better to break up new soils than to manure the old, America will either become a regular importer of manure, or will, without protecting duties, grow corn for herself only, and manufacturing for herself, will make her manure, as Mr. Carey desires, at home.*

For these obvious reasons, I hold Mr. Carey's economic arguments for Protectionism to be totally invalid. The economic, however, is far from being the strongest point of his case. American Protectionists often reason extremely ill; but it is an injustice to them to suppose that their Protectionist creed rests upon nothing superior to an economic blunder. Many of them have been led to it, much more by consideration for the higher interests of humanity, than by purely economic reasons. They, and Mr. Carey at their head, deem it a necessary condition of human improvement that towns should abound; that men should combine their labour, by means of interchange—with near neighbours, with people of pursuits, capacities, and mental cultivation different from their own, sufficiently close at hand for mutual sharpening of wits and enlarging of ideas—rather than with people on the opposite side of the globe. They believe that a nation all engaged in the same, or nearly the same, pursuit—a nation all agricultural—cannot attain a high state of civilization and culture. And for this there is a great foundation of reason. If the difficulty can be overcome, the United States, with their free institutions, their universal schooling, and their omnipresent

---

*[65] To this Mr. Carey would reply (indeed he has already so replied in advance) that of all commodities manure is the least susceptible of being conveyed to a distance. This is true of sewage, and of stable manure, but not true of the ingredients to which those manures owe their efficiency. These, on the contrary, are chiefly substances containing great fertilizing power in small bulk; substances of which the human body requires but a small quantity, and hence peculiarly susceptible of being imported; the mineral alkalies and the phosphates. The question indeed mainly concerns the phosphates, for of the alkalies, soda is procurable everywhere; while potass, being one of the constituents of granite and the other feldspathic rocks, exists in many subsoils, by whose progressive decomposition it is renewed, a large quantity also being brought down in the deposits of rivers. As for the phosphates, they, in the very convenient form of pulverized bones, are a regular article of commerce, largely imported into England; as they are sure to be into any country where the conditions of industry make it worth while to pay the price.

press, are the people to do it; but whether this is possible or not is still a problem. So far, however, as it is an object to check the excessive dispersion of the population, Mr. Wakefield has pointed out a better way; to modify the existing method of disposing of the unoccupied lands, by raising the price, instead of lowering it, or giving away the land gratuitously, as is largely done since the passing of the Homestead Act. To cut the knot in Mr. Carey's fashion, by Protectionism, it would be necessary that Ohio and Michigan should be protected against Massachusetts as well as against England: for the manufactories of New England, no more than those of the old country, accomplish his desideratum of bringing a manufacturing population to the doors of the Western farmer. Boston and New York do not supply the want of local towns to the Western prairies, any better than Manchester; and it is as difficult to get back the manure from the one place as from the other.

There is only one part of the Protectionist scheme which requires any further notice: its policy towards colonies, and foreign dependencies; that of compelling them to trade exclusively with the dominant country. A country which thus secures to itself an extra foreign demand for its commodities, undoubtedly gives itself some advantage in the distribution of the general gains of the commercial world. Since, however, it causes the industry and capital of the colony to be diverted from channels, which are proved to be the most productive, inasmuch as they are those into which industry and capital spontaneously tend to flow; there is a loss, on the whole, to the productive powers of the world, and the mother country does not gain so much as she makes the colony lose. If, therefore, the mother country refuses to acknowledge any reciprocity of obligation, she imposes a tribute on the colony in an indirect mode, greatly more oppressive and injurious than the direct. But if, with a more equitable spirit, she submits herself to corresponding restrictions for the benefit of the colony, the result of the whole transaction is the ridiculous one, that each party loses much, in order that the other may gain a little. V. W. Bladen and J. M. Robson (eds).

Collected Works of John Stuart Mill, Vol III, pp 911–22, University
of Toronto, 1965

21 G. R. Porter   The Progress of the Nation from the Beginning of the Nineteenth Century

The most famous of G. R. Porter's works was *The Progress of
the Nation from the Beginning of the Nineteenth Century*. The following passage is taken from the third edition of that work, published in 1851 as the Great Exhibition seemed to testify so
completely to the value of the free interchange of goods between the nations of the world.

We have happily now entered upon a course of legislation on
commercial subjects, which, when fully carried out, must realize
advantages in this direction which are more and more becoming
matters of necessity to this country. That the system of *free trade*,
by which expression is meant unrestricted intercourse with
foreign countries, in which no one country shall be placed, by
regulations or differential duties, at a disadvantage with any
other, and no Customs duty shall be levied for any purpose
whatever save the necessary one of revenue—a system in which
the fallacy of *protection* shall be utterly disowned and abolished—
that this system must be progressively carried out by us to its
utmost limit, is now seen to be among the most settled of cer-
tainties. To persons who have observed the effects of such relaxa-
tions in our tariff as have already been carried into effect, the
result of such a perfecting of the system as is here described cannot
be at all doubtful. That the capital, skill, and energy possessed
and exercised by the inhabitants of these islands will, when
unfettered, carry us forward to a degree of commercial and
manufacturing prosperity of which the world has hitherto seen
no example, it required little boldness to foretel; and, that this
prosperity will be attained to a very high degree, although the
example of England should fail to convince the governments of
other countries, and to be followed by them, does not admit of
any doubt. But it is not conceivable that our example, which, on

all other occasions has furnished motives of action, shall cease to do so, when seen to be fraught with so large a measure of good as hitherto has, and as no doubt will continue to accompany our course; and it cannot but add greatly to the feeling of gratification called forth by the changes now in progress, to believe that the sum of our prosperity shall be increased through the advancement of the general happiness. Shall we, then, too greatly flatter ourselves if we hope, that the nations of the world, too long divided by hatred in war, and jealousy in peace, shall be brought to see and act upon the conviction that the happiness and prosperity of each must tend to increase the happiness and prosperity of each and all other nations?

In seasons of general prosperity, when the productive classes are fully and profitably employed, it is always found that a stimulus is given to consumption, and it very frequently has happened that the effective demand for manufactured goods thus created has excited increased production to a degree beyond what has been immediately required. When circumstances change, and a check is given to consumption, those persons who have been led thus to apply an additional amount of capital and labour, are exposed to considerable losses, and it must be obvious that the danger of encountering the evil is greater in proportion as the market which they supply is circumscribed. If limited to one country, which is suffering under circumstances of depression, the distress of the producers must be highly aggravated, but if they are accustomed to carry on commercial dealings with many foreign lands, it is not probable that all will be at the same time under depression; the evil, as far as the producers are concerned, will be easily remedied, and a small reduction in the price of their goods will then cause such an increased demand in foreign countries as will greatly palliate, if it do not remedy, the mischief arising from fluctuations in the home demand.

If the view taken in these pages of our condition and prospects has any true foundation, it was quite impossible that the remaining branches of the restrictive system to which the legislature of this country so long and so pertinaciously adhered, could be much longer continued, and that we should still empower the comparatively few amongst us "who have obtained the proprietary possession of the soil, to increase artificially the money value of their estates," by means of a monopoly which threatened to be destructive of the happiness and social progress of the nation. The evils consequent upon persistance in a system of virtual exclusion were imminent; they were not of a nature to be put aside or delayed by temporising measures; it would, therefore, seem most in agreement with true wisdom at once to meet the difficulty, and to determine upon the adoption of a decisive change of system.

By following such a course, we must of necessity give full freedom to the productive industry of the country in all its branches, including among the rest that class for whose supposed benefit we so long submitted to a contrary system; for it would be absurd to suppose that in a state of things such as has here been contemplated, with a constantly increasing number of customers, our agriculturists must not share in the general prosperity, and that they should, under any circumstances, fail to obtain a return for their capital and labour equal to that realized by all other classes in the community: beyond this they can have no right to claim any advantage. G. R. Porter. *The Progress of the Nation from the Beginning of the Nineteenth Century*, 3rd ed, 1851

22 Rev Henry Dunckley   The Charter of the Nations

During the general election campaign of 1852 commercial policy again was in the forefront, and the Anti-Corn Law League reappeared on the scene briefly. A certain amount of money collected for its activities remained unexpended at the conclusion of the campaign, and part of this was used to stage an essay competition. The most successful entry was 'The Charter of the Nations' by the Rev Henry Dunckley, himself a keen Free Trader. In this book, which was published in 1854, Dunckley sang a song of triumph for his League paymasters.

It formed no part of the prescribed plan to enter, even incidentally, upon an argumentative vindication of Free Trade principles. However needful such a vindication may be abroad,
where the question has been scarcely at all discussed, it is unnecessary to say how obsolete it would have been here, after the
information which has been diffused through the exertions of the
Anti-Corn Law League. . . . The "Inquiry into the Wealth of
Nations" may be regarded as the forerunner of Free Trade,
and the firm hold which the principles of that work have now
taken of the popular mind, constitutes the safest guarantee that
ere long the last vestiges of Protection shall disappear from the
Statute Book. . . . There are now few persons who do not admit
that, as a mercantile people, it is our policy to allow our neighbours every possible opportunity of profitable trade, and that to
buy in the cheapest market the world affords, and to sell in the
dearest, is a natural right, as it is also the universal law of well-
being alike to individuals and communities . . . all laws which
aim at diverting trade from its natural channels; which step in
between the seller and the buyer, with a view to make them act
otherwise than a regard to their own interests would lead them
to act; nay, every species of impost which falls upon the process
of exchange, is essentially unjust, and at variance with the genius
of a free state . . . trade has now a chivalry of its own; a chivalry
whose stars are radiant with the more benignant lustre of justice,
happiness and religion, and whose titles will outlive the bar-
barous nomenclature of Charlemagne. Trade can be scorned no
longer; it has burst forth with the splendour of heaven-made
genius, and compelled the reluctant homage of all ranks. . . .
Industry now stood side by side with hereditary opulence; the
owner of ten thousand spindles confronted the lord of ten thousand acres; the one grasping the steam-engine, the other the
plough; each surrounded by an equal number of dependents,
and bearing an equal share in the burdens and dangers of the
state. Now the time has arrived when the shadow of an injustice
between such rivals could no longer be endured. . . . Trade shall
no longer pay a tribute to the soil . . . it would be just as reasonable

to accept the Ptolemaic system as the true philosophy of the heavens, or the physics of the schoolmen as a true exposition of the laws of nature, as to admit the theories of Protection in questions relating to industry and commerce. . . . Rev Henry Dunckley. Preface to 'The Charter of the Nations', League Prize Essay, 1854

23 William Ewart Gladstone   Speech in Parliament

It was the hope of Cobden, and many of his followers, that the British adoption of Free Trade would be imitated by other countries. Experience soon demonstrated that such hopes were ill founded. There were gleams of light, however, and perhaps the brightest of these was the Anglo-French Commercial Treaty of 1860, providing for substantial reciprocal tariff concessions between the two states. Cobden had taken a leading part in bringing about this treaty. This success, however, was a fleeting one, and the British example of Free Trade found little support in the commercial policies of other states in the latter part of the century.

This passage is taken from the major speech in which Gladstone, as Chancellor of the Exchequer, brought the provisions of the 1860 Treaty before the House of Commons.

These, then, are the principal stipulations of the Treaty with France, which may have been seen by hon. Members in one form or another, but which have not collectively, or upon authority, as yet met the public eye. I will not affect to be unaware that many objections have been stated to this Treaty. It has even been said that its terms indicate a subserviency to France, and involve a sacrifice of British interests to those of foreign nations or of a foreign Government. Sir, I am thankful to think that no Ministry, be its own merits or be the distinction of its chief what they may, can in this country hold office for a single Session upon terms of subserviency to any foreign Power whatever. There is here a perfect security (to omit all mention of any other guaran-

tees) in the nature and in the traditions of the two Houses of
Parliament. But, Sir, I know not what is meant by subserviency
to France as regards the articles of a Treaty like this. We have
given to France in the proper sense of the term, nothing by this
Treaty, if I except some very trifling fiscal sacrifice which we are
to make with respect to the single article of brandy. I mean that
it might not be necessary to reduce the duty to quite so low a
point as is fixed by the Treaty, and therefore there might be a
question whether some infinitesimal advantage may not be sur-
rendered in that form. But, with that small, and I believe solitary
exception, we have given nothing to France by this Treaty which
we have not given with as liberal a hand to ourselves. And the
changes here proposed are changes every one of which deserves
the acceptance of this House on its own merits, in conformity
with all the principles that have been recognized and acted upon
for many years past.

But further, Sir, as respects the charge of subserviency to
France, I know that this Treaty may be said to bear a political
character. The commercial relations of England with France
have always borne a political character. What is the history of
the system of prohibitions on the one side and on the other which
grew up between this country and France? It was simply this:—
That finding yourselves in political estrangement from her at the
time of the Revolution, you followed up and confirmed that
estrangement, both on the one side and the other, by a system
of prohibitory duties. And I do not deny that it was effectual for
its end. I do not mean for its economical end. Economically it
may, I admit, have been detrimental enough to both countries;
but for its political end it was effectual. And because it was
effectual I call upon you to legislate now for an opposite end by
the exact reverse of that process. And if you desire to knit together
in amity those two great nations whose conflicts have often
shaken the world, undo for your purpose that which your fathers
did for their purpose, and pursue with equal intelligence and
consistency an end that is more beneficial. Sir, there was once
a time when close relations of amity were established between

the Governments of England and France. It was in the reign of
the later Stuarts; and it marks a dark spot in our annals, because
it was an union formed in a spirit of domineering ambition on
the one side, and of base and vile subserviency on the other. But
that, Sir, was not an union of the nations; it was an union of the
Governments. This is not to be an union of the Governments;
it is to be an union of the nations; and I confidently say again,
as I have already ventured to say in this House, that there never
can be any union between the nations of England and France
except an union beneficial to the world, because directly either
the one or the other begins to harbour schemes of selfish aggran-
dizement, that moment the jealousy of its neighbour will power-
fully react, and the very fact of their being in harmony will of
itself be at all times the most conclusive proof that neither of them
can meditate anything which is dangerous to Europe.

There is another class of objections of which I do not complain,
but which I hope to remove. There are those who say that a
commercial treaty is an abandonment of the principles of free
trade. Well, certainly a commercial treaty would be an abandonment of the principles of free trade, in the latitude in which we
now employ that phrase, if it involved the recognition of exclusive privileges. In this sense I admit that Mr. Pitt's commercial treaty would, if we had now adopted it in the terms in
which it was expressed, have been on our part an abandonment
of free trade; but, at the same time, I cannot mention that treaty
without saying that I think it was, for the time at which it was
made, one of the best and one of the wisest measures ever adopted
by Parliament, and has contributed at least as much as any other
passage of his brilliant career to the fame of the great statesman
who concluded it. We, however, have no exclusive engagements;
we have not the pretence of an exclusive engagement. France is
perfectly aware that our legislation makes no distinction between
one nation and another, and that what we enact for her we shall
at the same time enact for all the world.

I am, however, a little surprised at the number and variety of
these objections which come rushing from all quarters. It is like

the ancient explanation of the physical cause of a storm—all the winds, north, east, west, and south, rushing together:—

> "Unà Eurusque Notusque ruunt, creberque procellis
>   Africus."

Sometimes a treaty is an obsolete and antiquated idea; sometimes it is a dangerous innovation. In the view of one class it is an abandonment of free trade. There are also another class of men, of opinions diametrically at variance with these, and those are gentlemen with whom we shall have much difficulty in dealing. These are they who find fault with it—and that I must say is by far the soundest objection, inasmuch as it is unquestionably founded on the facts—because it is an abandonment of the principle of protection. This treaty is an abandonment of the principle of protection. I am not aware of any entangling engagement which it contains; it certainly contains no exclusive privilege, but it is an abandonment of the principle of protection, and a means, I hope complete and efficacious, of sweeping from the statute book the chief relics of that miscalled system which still remain upon it. The fact is, and you will presently see that it is so, that our old friend Protection, who used formerly to dwell in the palaces of the land, and who was dislodged from them some ten or fifteen years ago, has since that period found very comfortable shelter and good living in holes and corners; and you are now invited, if you will have the goodness to concur in the operation, to see whether you cannot likewise eject him from those holes and corners. I told you that we are to remove the duty from all manufactured goods. Now, Sir, there is hardly one of that class of duties which is not, in point of fact, the representative of a strictly protective duty; nay more—and mark my words—in many cases of a prohibitory duty.

Perhaps the best method of giving a summary view of the case will be by my stating to the Committee what will be the financial results of the treaty as it stands. I will not enter into any of the smaller details, and will take three branches of reduction only— the reduction of the duty upon wine, the reduction of that upon brandy, and the abolition of the duties upon manufactured goods. The reduction of the duty upon wine from 5s. 10d. to 3s. per gallon will afford to the consumer a relief of £830,000, and will entail upon the revenue, after allowing for an increase of consumption to the extent of 35 per cent, a loss of £515,000. The reduction of the duty upon brandy from 15s. to 8s. 2d. a gallon will give to the consumer a relief of £446,000, and, assuming that the consumption will be raised to the point at which it stood in 1850, just before the disease of the vine commenced, it will cause a loss of £225,000 to the revenue. Before I give the chief items of manufactured goods I will mention some minor cases, with which we propose to deal for the time as exceptions. There are three small articles the abolition of the duties on which we propose to postpone for a short period, in the meantime reducing it by one-half. One of them is the article cork, which has been the subject of a great deal of debate in this House. I must say that although there never was a stronger apparent case made out for protection, and although, in consequence of the measures which were adopted, there has been a considerable shock to the trade, and a considerable change of its nature and of the course which it takes, the House has nothing to repent. On the contrary, the total consumption of cork wood in the domestic manufacture is much larger now than it was before the duty was reduced. On account of the importance of the present change, however, we propose to give until the 1st of April, 1861, for the reduction of the duty on cork; and we also propose a delay of the changes affecting two other trades, upon the simple ground that they are trades carried on almost entirely by widely-diffused rural labour, to which it is not desirable to give a sudden shock. These are the glove trade and the trade in straw plaiting. In the meantime the duties will be reduced, and next year they will be taken off.

I pass now to state the mode in which the treaty deals with manufactured goods in general. The amount of duty on these articles, which will be abolished, is no less than £432,000. The principal articles are silk manufactures, £270,000; gloves, subject to a short delay, £48,000; artificial flowers, £20,000; watches, £15,000; certain oils, £10,000; musical instruments,

£9,000; leather, £9,000; china, £8,000; glass, £7,000, and many others yielding smaller amounts. There are a great number of minor articles of industry produced largely in France, especially in Paris. The total relief to the consumer—that is the gross amount of duty remitted under the French treaty—will be £1,737,000; the loss to the revenue for the first year will probably be £1,190,000. Now, Sir, the objections which are taken to this treaty in the interests of Free Trade will not, I am quite sure, be very long-lived; but there is one objection which turns upon another point, and with which I must endeavour to deal. It is that which tells us that the duties we are about to repeal are, forsooth, revenue duties, and duties which are levied upon luxuries, but which do not affect the poor man. Compassion for the poor man is a very fine feeling, and I should be very sorry to say anything that appeared to depreciate or undervalue so sacred a sentiment, but I must say that it is entirely out of place here. There is not one of these duties that is a revenue duty—no, not one of them. How they work with respect to poor men, how they work with respect to those who are not rich men, we will presently inquire. But if these are revenue duties, it is very curious to notice which are the classes that are alarmed at the treaty. Are the manufacturers of British brandy the guardians of the British revenue? Are the importers of Cape wines the guardians of the British revenue? Have the manufacturers of British wines a peculiar interest in the well-being of the exchequer? The manufacturers of Spitalfields, and those of Coventry, who have an incomparable organ in my right hon. Friend (Mr. Ellice), are most excellent citizens, and no doubt contribute their share to the revenue; but my right hon. Friend will not tell me that their great activity, their speed in rushing up to London, and urging their representations upon this subject, has arisen from their interest in the British revenue. It has arisen from something very different. These gentlemen do not enter my room to tell me that they come there as the guardians of the British revenue; they tell a much more simple and a much more intelligible tale. They say this—that the duties which now stand upon your tariff are, and it is perfectly true, levied upon articles consumed by the rich. But why are they not levied upon articles consumed by the middle, the lower middle class, and the poor? Because they will not let them in; because they are prohibitory as against those articles. That is the explanation of the whole case. Our manufacturers give over to France the highest qualities under cover of duties, which are as good for their purpose as prohibitions, and reserve for themselves the making of the lower qualities, and the power of exacting from the British consumer a higher price than they will be able to obtain if this treaty is confirmed by Parliament. I took the liberty of saying to one of the deputations, "It seems to me this is much the case of the corn law over again." Now do not let there be any mistake. What is wanted is, a higher price than that at which the public can get goods from France. That is the Alpha and Omega, the beginning and the end of it. I asked then, "Is not this the case of the corn law?" The answer was, "Oh dear, no; not the least like the corn law." In fact, there is generally, on the part of the most respectable classes, a desire for the protection of their own business. They show that though they are without exception adherents of free trade, they are not adherents of free trade without exception. They make no secret of it, nor should there be any secret made of it here, that the duties in which they take an interest are not revenue duties but are protection duties, and, therefore, duties ill adapted for the purposes of revenue.

Let us now, Sir, proceed to consider some of the circumstances which have rendered it allowable and desirable, in the view of Her Majesty's advisers, to make a special arrangement in this case. I entreat the Committee to look at the present state of the trade between England and France; it is not a little instructive. Consider, in the first place, the relative positions of England and France. It is perfectly true, that France is a foreign country, but she is a foreign country separated from you absolutely by a narrower channel than that which divides you from Ireland; and while nature, or Providence rather, has placed you in the closest proximity, it has also given to these two great countries such

diversities of soil, climate, products, and character, that I do not
believe you can find, on the face of the world, two other countries
which are so constituted for carrying on a beneficial and extended
commerce. I believe, indeed, that the prohibitory system sub-
sisting between England and France is but little less unnatural
as to every commercial—I think I may add as to every moral and
political—result than if you were to revive those prohibitory
systems which formerly separated England from Scotland, and
Great Britain from Ireland. I shall be told, perhaps, that our
system is not prohibitory. And certainly in respect of many
articles the statement is a true one, for we have considerable
importations from France; but when I remember how much we
still practically prohibit, I have no hesitation in saying that,
although our system is far better than that of France, yet, on the
other hand, it is far indeed from being what it ought to be. And
now let us look for a moment at the question on the French side.
The doctrine is that we should attend to our own interests, and
leave France to manage hers. What, then, is the state of the trade
as regards France? In 1858 the total value of exports from
England to France—not British exports only, but exports of
whatever origin—was £14,821,000. Of that amount the home
consumption in France took £10,465,000. A portion of the
articles are unenumerated, and I cannot get at the details, but
I have obtained the particulars of articles to the value of
£9,819,000, about nineteen-twentieths of the whole. Observe
how they are distributed. Of this large proportion of the goods
sent to France in 1858, amounting to £9,819,000, raw materials,
upon which no labour whatever had been employed, and the
great bulk of which were not of British origin, but merely passed
through our warehouses, were £8,070,000, and half-manufac-
tured articles were £1,060,000. The total amount of manufactures which we send abroad every year is about £130,000,000;
but in 1858 our exports of manufactured goods to France were
only £688,000. It is worth while to go yet one step further in the
analysis. Of that £688,000, £208,000 were for Cashmere shawls,
which merely came here in transit, and £217,000 for machinery,

which our friends over the water have been pleased to admit under some notion of special advantage. The value of all the other manufactured articles sent from the United Kingdom to France was £263,000. I want to know whether that is a state of things so satisfactory that when we have an opportunity of amending it we should refuse to do so. I understand the statement of the moderate Free Trader who says that half a loaf is better than no bread, that all breaking down of restrictions is good, and that it is wiser to break down our own restrictions and leave those of our neighbour standing if we cannot touch them than to perpetuate both. That is true and reasonable; but I cannot understand those immoderate and unmanageable Free Traders who come from other quarters, many of whom have not long been thus fastidious and jealous on behalf of free trade in its most rigid purity, and who seem to think it is a positive evil to induce our neighbours to break down their restrictions. They do not see that what they condemn is a doubling of the benefit. They think there is a chivalry in free trade, which is degraded if it becomes a matter of bargain, whereas it appears to me that bargain is really the true end and aim of the whole. The only reason why we have not made bargains similar to the present in former years was simply because we could not make them. It was not for want of trying. For four or five years this was almost the chief business of one or more departments of the State, and yet no progress could be made. Why? Because they set out upon a false principle —the principle that the concessions which each party made to the other were not a benefit but an injury to itself. We have not proceeded upon that principle. We have never pretended to France that we were going to inflict injury upon ourselves. Hansard's *Parliamentary Debates*, 3rd Series, Vol CLVI, col 835–42, 10 February 1860

24 Charles Kingsley   Letter

Not everyone was convinced that Free Trade was an unmixed blessing. The Christian Socialists of the third quarter of the century, who wanted British society to be based on the responsibilities and duties entailed by true Christianity rather than on the materialistic and individualistic theories that they conceived Cobdenism to entail, were among the doubters. Both Kingsley and Maurice were Anglican clergymen, and both took a sincere interest in social questions. Maurice played an important part in schemes to improve working-class education, while Kingsley, in his novels, tried to arouse the conscience of contemporaries to the social ills of the day.

The Kingsley letter quoted here refers to the political affairs of 1852. On the collapse of Lord John Russell's Whig government a minority Conservative administration headed by Lord Derby had taken office, with no clear enunciation of its major policies, especially on commerce. During the general election campaign the League was dramatically resurrected, and though the government made gains, a Free Trade majority was returned. Derby's government was obliged in the new session of 1852 to swallow a Free Trade resolution, but this did not save it, for it was beaten on Disraeli's Budget at the end of the year and resigned.

———

... Next you have the Manchester school, from whom Heaven defend us; for of all narrow, conceited, hypocritical, and anarchic and atheistic schemes of the universe, the Cobden and Bright one is exactly the worst. I have no language to express my contempt for it, and therefore I quote what Maurice wrote to me this morning. 'If the Ministry would have thrown Protection to the dogs (as I trust they have, in spite of the base attempts of the Corn Law Leaguers to goad them to committing themselves to it, and to hold them up as the people's enemies), and thrown themselves into social measures, who would not have clung to them, to avert the horrible catastrophe of a Manchester ascendancy, which I believe in my soul would be fatal to intellect, morality, and freedom, and will be more likely to move a rebellion among the working men than any Tory rule which can be conceived.'

Of course it would. To pretend to be the workmen's friends, by keeping down the price of bread, when all they want thereby is to keep down wages and increase profits, and in the meantime to widen the gulf between the working man and all that is time-honoured, refined, and chivalrous in English society, that they may make the men their divided slaves, that is—perhaps half unconsciously, for there are excellent men amongst them—the game of the Manchester school. . . . From a letter written by Charles Kingsley in 1852, and cited by Thomas Hughes in his 'Prefatory Memoir' to Kingsley's *Alton Locke*

PART FOUR

Early Challenges to Free Trade—Fair Trade, Tariff Reform and Mr Baldwin

The general prosperity of the third quarter of the century was held to justify a Free Trade policy, and it was not until the slump of the late 1870s that ideas of tariff reform reappeared. A sharp but temporary depression then was accompanied by more deep-seated and long-lived difficulties for British agriculture. It became clear also from the growth of the German and American economies that Britain's proud role of 'the workshop of the world' was not immutable. Politically, the international balance of power was altered by the emergence of Bismarck's Germany. These developments fostered the first notable challenge to Free Trade, the Fair Trade movement. The two main factors in this agitation were imperial sentiment, more obvious then in some of the colonies than at home, and the reaction of those industries which found themselves hard hit by foreign competition. From parts of the West Riding, in particular, in the 1880s came sharp attacks on Free Trade. The Fair Trade movement wanted to abandon it for a free hand in commercial policy. Imperial preference would be revived, in order to improve imperial unity and strengthen the international position of the Empire, while the imposition of tariffs—or the threat to impose them—would be used to defend the British share of international trade.

For a while in the early 1880s it seemed possible that Fair Trade might be adopted by the Conservative Party; however, the need to maintain the broadest possible unity among those opposed to Gladstone's Home Rule policy made such a divisive commercial programme impolitic. The Liberal Unionists were still Free Traders, and the Conservative flirtation with Fair Trade proved short-lived. An example of Fair Trade argument is given here (25) together with a trenchant repudiation by Gladstone of such commercial heresy (26).

A more serious challenge to Free Trade came in 1903. Joseph Chamberlain embarked on his Tariff Reform crusade, with the main idea of producing an imperial economic union based on mutual tariff concessions between the colonies and the mother country. This would buttress the international position of the British Empire, and tie it more closely together, while at the same time financing social reform at home. Chamberlain began this campaign in May 1903 (27), and a few months later resigned from Balfour's Unionist cabinet in order to have a free hand in fighting the battle against Free Trade. The immediate political consequences were disastrous, for the raising of the banner of Tariff Reform broke the unity of the Unionist coalition, while it united Liberals and Labour in defence of the Cobdenite tradition. It is, for example, scarcely surprising that the Lancashire Conservatives, an important element in that party's strength, tended to be very unhappy about a policy which might eventually impede the free import of raw cotton or lead to retaliation against British exports. Chamberlain succeeded in obtaining a good deal of support—especially from imperialists and from those economic interests which felt the need for protection most strongly. Others, however, would not abandon the commercial policy under which Britain had gained so much (28).

If then Tariff Reform broke the Unionist front, it had a precisely opposite effect on the opposition forces. The Liberal party had been in the doldrums since the Home Rule split, and emerged from the Boer War in obvious disarray, but defence of Free Trade was a platform on which almost all Liberals could enthusiastically unite. Asquith took the lead as Chamberlain's principal opponent (29).

The Liberals were joined in this policy by the infant Labour party, which had not as yet worked out its own economic doctrines (30). Moreover, most professional economists were still committed to Free Trade (31).

As in the crisis over the Corn Laws half a century earlier, the political battle was not carried on entirely on a plane of high economic argument, and cruder propaganda of many kinds played a part (32–6). The decisive moment in this struggle came with the general election of 1906, when the Liberals and their allies won a crushing victory, and Free Trade was saved for the time being.

The next serious challenge did not come until after the First World War. In the general election of 1922, following the fall of Lloyd George, the new prime minister, Bonar Law, though a tariff reformer himself, promised for tactical reasons that he would not abandon Free Trade without a clear mandate for that purpose from the electorate. When Baldwin succeeded Bonar Law a few months later, he decided that a change in commercial policy was essential, and that the pledge given by his predecessor was binding (37). A sudden dissolution at the end of 1923 saw Liberals and Labour again united in defence of Free Trade (38–40).

Once again tariff reform was defeated, and Baldwin's defeat brought in the first Labour government. The strength of Free Trade sentiment at this time can be seen by the way which the opponents of Free Trade avoided the word 'protection' and fought usually under more innocent-sounding slogans like Fair Trade or Tariff Reform. The victory of 1923, however, was Free Trade's last great success; it had less than a decade to endure as the main plank in Britain's economic policy.

25 Lord Penzance   Collapse of the Free Trade Argument

Lord Penzance (James P. Wilde, 1816–99) was a distinguished

commercial and ecclesiastical lawyer and judge. In the 1860s
as a moderate Liberal he played an important part in legal and
religious reform. Like many other moderate Liberals of the
period he was unable to remain true to the pure Gladstonian
line. The Home Rule crisis of 1886 saw him on the Liberal
Unionist side, but as this document shows he had already
fallen into commercial heresy. The passage is taken from an
article in *The Nineteenth Century*, then an influential periodical,
and it provides a good example of Fair Trade argument.

Will the lion always continue to possess his share? Does not
that depend on how he conducts himself? The advance of other
nations into those regions of manufacture in which we used to
stand either alone or supreme, should make us alive to the
possible future. Where we used to find customers we now find
rivals, and with a magnanimous disdain for all rivalry we sell to
all comers our coal, the source of mechanical power, and our
machinery, the means by which that mechanical power may be
profitably exerted. Prudence is not alarm, and prudence demands a dispassionate inquiry into the course we are pursuing,
in place of a blind adhesion to a discredited theory. That such
an inquiry can be long delayed I do not believe.

At any rate, let us hope that we have heard the last of the
shibboleth that every import necessitates a corresponding export
of British goods. The advocate of the Cobden Club has abandoned it as untenable, substituting for it the undeniable truth
that all foreign goods are paid for by something of equal value.

In like manner must be abandoned the belief that our prosperity since 1846 is due to Free Trade; for this belief can only
be supported upon the assumption that, because we are still at
the head of nations in commercial prosperity, as we always have
been, therefore the system of free imports which we have acted
upon for the last forty years must be sound, although we enjoyed
the same pre-eminence at a time when we acted upon the
opposite system of Protection.

On these two questions, then, the Free Trade contention as

I

expounded by the chosen champion of the Cobden Club is a complete collapse. Does the Committee of the Cobden Club offer us anything else in support of the Free Trade faith? Absolutely nothing. There is no mysterious merit in the background, or surely their able champion, Mr. Medley, would have disclosed it. Let the artisan, then, who suffers from the injury or extinction of his industry—let the employer of labour who suffers from a system under which large portions of our wealth, as fast as it is acquired, are poured into the lap of foreign countries in the shape of wages for the support of their populations, while our own people are craving for work, look this system in the face.

Let them bear in mind that neither Europe nor America— monarchies nor republics—contains a community which does not repudiate it. The injuries it inflicts are patent and notorious and are forced under our eyes alike in the statistics of trade and the records of the daily press.

What are the benefits that counterbalance them?

The supporters of 'Free Imports' have been challenged to point them out, and, so far as Mr. Medley's essay is concerned, have miserably failed to do so.

Is it anything short of infatuation, then, to defer inquiry until the mischief is done? It takes a long time to displace the commerce and established manufactures which have been built up by the patient energy of past generations, and are still upheld by the wealth and industry of such a country as Great Britain; and the inroad made upon us under the shelter of our own laws may not as yet have reached formidable dimensions. But is that a sensible reason for refusing to inquire whether our system is sound or not? The road you are travelling may be the wrong one, though your foot is not yet in the morass to which it leads. Your mode of life may be unhealthy, though your health is not yet seriously impaired. Many causes, and notably the civil war in America and the Franco-German struggle in Europe, have combined to sustain our commerce since Free Trade was adopted by checking the progress of those who are now our rivals, and reducing the effects of competition. But these countervailing incidents are little likely to be repeated. All prudence then points one way, but unfortunately two great national characteristics point the other. First, that noble tenacity of purpose which makes us hold fast to whatever position we have taken up; that refuses to acknowledge defeat, and elevates persistence into a virtue; and next, the curse of Ethelred the Unready, which ever tempts us to defer the moment of defence to the moment of actual disaster. . . .

. . . The hope I spoke of is already, I believe, on the road to fulfilment. We cannot shut our eyes to the fast-growing desire which has lately sprung up for the welding of our magnificent colonies into a real Empire with these islands. The time is opportune, the colonies are favourable, and we have a statesman at the head of affairs who has given effective proofs that he regards the national welfare above the miserable interests of party warfare— a statesman whose commanding genius is capable of grasping this vast question and guiding these national aspirations to a fruitful end. How long, then, after these islands and our colonies become knit together for offence and defence, for mutual dependence and support, shall we be content to draw our supplies of food from Russia, from Spain, or the United States? How long, indeed, shall we be able to refuse to our brethren and fellow-subjects whatever advantage over the foreigner our fiscal laws can secure to them without laying an undue burden on the consumer in this country?

And a further question—Is it not to be expected that treatment of this kind may be demanded by our colonies as the reasonable basis upon which alone they will be content to unite their fortunes and their future with ours? Lord Penzance. 'Collapse of the Free Trade Argument', *The Nineteenth Century*, Vol XX, No 2, 1886

26 William Ewart Gladstone Speech at Leeds

Gladstone never wavered in his commitment to the Free Trade gospel. While in the early 1880s many Conservative leaders, including Lord Salisbury himself, seemed to be wavering, he stood firm. Fair Trade agitation was strong in these years in parts of the West Riding, but in this major policy speech at Leeds in October 1881 Gladstone made his position unmistakable.

. . . The principal seat of this depression is not to be looked for in the pressure of foreign tariffs, though that is a very serious subject, but it is to be looked for in bad harvests. . . . But, gentlemen, in reference to this subject of the depression of trade, an attempt is made to raise a great and most mischievous delusion. An institution has been formed in the imposing name of the Fair Trade League. What in the world, you will ask, does that mean? Well, gentlemen, I must say it bears a suspicious likeness to our old friend Protection. (Cheers and laughter.) Protection was dead and buried 30 years ago, but he has come out of the grave and is walking in the broad light of day, but after long experience of the atmosphere underground, he endeavours to look somewhat more attractive than he used to appear . . . and in consequence he found it convenient to assume a new name. (Laughter.) . . . can you strike the foreigner hard by retaliatory tariffs? What manufactures do you import from abroad? In all £45,000,000. What manufactures do you export? Nearer £200,000,000 (cheers)—over £200,000,000. If you are to make the foreigner feel, you must make him feel by striking him in his largest interests; but the interests which he has in sending manufactures to you is one of his smallest interests, and you are invited to inflict wounds upon yourself in a field measured by £45,000,000, while he has got exactly the same power of inflicting wounds upon you on a field measured by more than £200,000,000. . . . The Americans hit us very hard in their duties, and there is a great reduction, no doubt, in our exports to America. But still, how do they stand? America sends to us less than £3,000,000 of manufactured goods; we send to America, what between our own manufactured goods, and the foreign produce which we have got for our manufactured goods, between £30,000,000 and £40,000,000 of manufactured goods, notwithstanding; and now the advice of these fair traders is that we are to endeavour, by hitting America through this £3,000,000 which she sends to us, to make her cease from hitting us through the 30 odd millions we send her. (Cheers). It is impossible that absurdity can further go. (Cheers).... This is a very serious question indeed. A quarter of a century of the legislative life of this country was occupied in the solution of this great problem. (Cheers).... It was nearly a generation of the life of the nation that we gave to it, and almost everything else was cast aside in the legislation of those years, and you will find that little was done except this one memorable, conspicuous, and, I may almost say, incomparable triumph; for a triumph more beneficent, either materially or morally, to the interests of men I believe never was attained by public virtue or public intelligence. (Loud cheers.) ... What I now say is this— that the thought that this question can be disposed of by taxing foreign manufactures is a thing to my mind perfectly ludicrous. (Loud cheers.) ... This is a question that vitally touches our national existence.... It is certainly a subject upon which those who lead British citizens should above all others know their own minds. I have told you, and I hope I have told you intelligibly, what my mind is. I will be no party to unsettling at its top or its bottom one single stone of the noble structure which was reared by the combined efforts of many able men, and most of all by the efforts of Mr. Cobden and Mr. Bright, (cheers), for which many of us have laboured, for which some of us have suffered, but by which the land has prospered, and to which the people of the country have given their solemn and final adherence. (Loud and prolonged cheering.) *The Times*, 8 October 1881

27 Joseph Chamberlain Speech at Birmingham

Joseph Chamberlain began his political career with the narrow radical politics of militant Dissent, but broke with Gladstone over Home Rule and took his Liberal Unionist followers over into the Unionist camp. He served as Colonial Secretary in Salisbury's last government and in Balfour's government. He felt increasingly that greater imperial unity was imperative.

The help given by the colonies to the mother country during
the Boer War enhanced his faith in the possibility of this
greater unity. He tried to convert Balfour's cabinet to this
view, and when he found these efforts unavailing he determined to speak out publicly. This passage is taken from the
major speech delivered in Birmingham on 15 May 1903 in
which Chamberlain inaugurated his campaign for Tariff
Reform and imperial unity.

. . . How do you think that under such circumstances we can
approach our colonies with appeals to aid us in promoting the
unity of the Empire, or ask them to bear a share of the common
burden? Are we to say to them, "This is your Empire, take pride
in it, share its privileges." They say—"What are its privileges?
The privileges appear to be if we treat you as relations and
friends; if we show you kindness, we give you preference, you who
benefit by our action can only leave us alone to fight our own
battles against those who are offended by our action." Now is
that free trade? (Cries of "No".) . . . No, it is absolutely a new
situation. (Cheers.) There has been nothing like it in our history.
It was a situation which was never contemplated by any of those
whom we regard as the authors of free trade. What would Mr.
Bright, what would Mr. Cobden, have said to this state of things?
I do not know. It would be presumptuous to imagine; but this
I can say. Mr. Cobden did not hesitate to make a treaty of
reciprocity and preference with France (hear, hear), and Mr.
Bright did not hesitate to approve his action; and I cannot
believe if they had been present among us now and known what
this new situation was, I cannot believe that they would have
hesitated to make a treaty of preference and reciprocity with our
own children. (Loud and prolonged cheers.) Well, you see the
point. You want an Empire. (Hear, hear.) Do you think it better
to cultivate the trade with your own people or to let that go in
order that you may keep the trade of those who, rightly enough,
are your competitors and rivals? I say it is a new position. I say
the people of this Empire have got to consider it. I do not want

to hasten their decision. They have two alternatives before them. They may maintain if they like in all its severity the interpretation, in my mind an entirely artificial and wrong interpretation, which has been placed upon the doctrine of free trade by a small remnant of Little Englanders of the Manchester school who now profess to be the sole repositories of the doctrines of Mr. Cobden and Mr. Bright. They may maintain that policy in all its severity, although it is repudiated by every other nation and by all your own colonies. In that case they will be absolutely precluded either from giving any kind of preference or favour to any of their colonies abroad or even protecting their colonies abroad when they offer to favour us. That is the first alternative. The second alternative is that we should insist that we will not be bound by any purely technical definition of free trade, that, while we seek as one chief object free interchange of trade and commerce between ourselves and all the nations of the world, we will nevertheless recover our freedom, resume that power of negotiation, and if, necessary, retaliation, (loud cheers), whenever our own interests or our relations between our colonies and ourselves are threatened by other people. (Cheers.) I leave the matter in your hands. I desire that a discussion on this subject should be opened. The time has not yet come to settle it; but it seems to me that for good or evil this is an issue much greater in its consequences than any of our local disputes. (Hear, hear.) Make a mistake in legislation, yet it can be corrected; make a mistake in your Imperial policy, it is irretrievable. You have an opportunity; you will never have it again. . . . *The Times*, 16 May 1903

28 Winston Spencer Churchill Letter of Resignation to Balfour

The immediate result of Chamberlain's pronouncement was to split the Unionist coalition that had dominated British politics since the Home Rule crisis of the mid-1880s. Among those who would not swallow Tariff Reform, or even Balfour's attempts at compromise, was the young Winston Churchill, at that time a promising backbench MP. His father, Lord Randolph Churchill, had combined a belief in the need for the Conservatives to appeal to popular opinion with a determination as Chancellor of the Exchequer to show that a Conservative government could be as rigidly economical as Gladstone himself. His son, never perhaps outstandingly knowledgeable about economic questions, however great his other qualities, refused to follow Joseph Chamberlain into economic heresy in 1903. Instead, when it became clear that Balfour would not repudiate Tariff Reform entirely, Churchill crossed the floor of the House to join the defenders of Free Trade.

---

25 May 1903
Most Private

Dear Mr Balfour,

You have shown me so much kindness in the past that I am encouraged to write to you frankly now about Mr Chamberlain's recent statements; & indeed the matter seems to me so important that it is my duty to do so.

At Birmingham he advocated Preferential Tariffs with the Colonies; in his letter of Monday to a Mr Loveday he revealed plain Protectionist intentions; & in the House on Friday last he showed himself prepared to use Old Age Pensions as a lever to attain these ends. Now I see it stated by Mr Bonar Law that you are agreed with him in all this.

I earnestly hope this is not true & that you have not taken an irrevocable decision. Hence this letter.

I am utterly opposed to anything which will alter the Free Trade character of this country; & I consider such an issue superior in importance to any other now before us. Preferential Tariffs, even in respect of articles wh we are bound to tax for revenue purposes, are dangerous & objectionable. But of course it is quite impossible to stop there and I am persuaded that once this policy is begun it must lead to the establishment of a complete Protective system, involving commercial disaster, & the Americanisation of English politics. I do not now attempt to argue all this. But I submit these two points to you.

1. From a national point of view there is no case for a fiscal resolution: not in the Trade Returns, nor Income Tax receipts, nor in a colonial demand, nor in a popular movement.

2. From a party point of view: the government is probably less unpopular than any which has ruled 8 years in England. Their record—army & expenditure apart—will make a fine page in history. They have no reason to dread an appeal to the constituencies; & even if a general election should result in a transference of power, the conservative party would be in a strong minority quite able to protect those causes & institutions which they cherish. In five or six years a healthy operation of opinion would recall them once more to power. Why is it necessary to play such desperate stakes?

I feel perhaps that I may have sometimes been the cause of embarrassment to the government. It is difficult to write about such things because of obvious rejoinders, but I should like to tell you that an attempt on your part to preserve the Free Trade policy & character of the Tory party would command my absolute loyalty. I would even swallow six army corps—if it would make any difference & sink all minor differences. But if on the other hand you have made up your mind & there is no going back, I must reconsider my position in politics. Please do not consider this letter disrespectful or anything but a statement of fact. I should be very sorry to cause you annoyance of any kind. But after all you ought to know how seriously some of us regard this great question

Yours vy sincerely
WINSTON S. CHURCHILL

Randolph S. Churchill. *Winston S. Churchill*, Vol II, pp 58–9, London, 1967

---

29 H. H. Asquith Speech at Largo, Fife

If the consequences of Chamberlain's revolt were to be disastrous for the Unionists, for the Liberals it was a life-line.

Defence of Free Trade reunited the divergent sections into which the party had clearly been divided during the Boer war. Among those who gained markedly during the period between May 1903 and the general election victory of 1906 was H. H. Asquith (1852–1928), who took the lead as Chamberlain's main opponent in public controversy. *The Times* summarises part of Asquith's speech at Largo, Fife, on 16 October 1903

If they looked back to the condition of the country as a whole under protection, and compared it with the condition of the people today, they would find not only an indisputable, but almost incalculable, progress. The country was richer, the capitalists were better off, the labour classes had gained proportionately even more than any other class. They had more wages, more regular employment, and fewer periods of depression; and, what was even more important, every shilling they received by way of wages had a much larger purchasing power over the commodities which made up the comforts and even the luxuries of life. There were no other means by which they could maintain the comfort of the people and the prosperity and progress of their commerce both at home and in the foreign markets than by securing the freest and fullest possible influx into these islands of the food and raw materials which were the very basis of our industry. It was on these grounds, and not from any pedantic devotion to any abstract principle or policy, but on grounds of common sense and experience, that he appealed to them not to sacrifice the great blessings free trade had conferred upon them. .... *The Times*, 17 October 1903

30 Labour Representation Committee Policy Statement 1906

A feature of the first years of the twentieth century was the rise of the Labour Party. The Labour Representation Committee was founded in 1900, in not very impressive circumstances. In the next few years it scored one or two notable bye-election victories, then adverse legal decisions, especially the Taff Vale case, gave it more and more trade-union support as a body that could mobilise political strength and eventually change the law to safeguard the position of the unions. An obvious tactic was to seek an alliance between Liberals and Labour against the Unionist government. The LRC had not thought out its own economic policies at this time, and fought shy of any socialist label. In these circumstances it could readily join in the defence of Free Trade. As early as 1903 an agreement had been reached between Ramsay MacDonald and the Liberal Chief Whip, Herbert Gladstone, for an informal alliance against the Unionists when the general election came along. The general election of 1906 saw a major growth of Labour representation and the formation of the parliamentary Labour Party. The document reproduced here is one of the policy statements produced by the LRC in the campaign for this general election, and shows the Labour commitment to the defence of Free Trade, and the way in which that commitment was justified to Labour supporters.

Labour Representation Leaflets.—No. 10.

UNITED LABOUR MANIFESTO

ON

TARIFFS

AND

LABOUR CONDITIONS.

To the Trade Unionists of Great Britain and Ireland—

After sixty years of a Free Trade policy the country is being asked to return to Protection, and one of the chief reasons given for the change is, that work will thereby become more plentiful and that wages will thereby be increased. If these results would follow, every Trade Unionist should vote for Protection.

IS PROTECTION A REMEDY?

We have, however, the experience of the whole industrial world to guide us. The present state of our trade is bad—trade is always bad after a war—and the outlook is rather gloomy. But in Protected Germany the demands of the unemployed are as pressing as they are here; in Protected America the number of business failures is greater in proportion than in Free Trade England. Therefore we see that unemployment and bad trade are at least as severe under Protection as under Free Trade.

DO IMPORTS IMPOVERISH US?

It seems, at first sight, as though the amount of goods we are purchasing from abroad is a cause of unemployment at home. No doubt some trades suffer by open ports. But this question must not be considered from a narrow local or trade point of view. The trades that have suffered from open ports are those which cannot be carried on economically under British conditions. They can only succeed by impoverishing the wage-earners in other industries. Taking the whole amount of our national trade into account, it cannot be said that that amount would be increased by Protection, because we pay for our imports by the services we render to the foreigner. If we ceased to buy we should cease to sell. Consequently, the small local benefits which Protection may confer will be much more than counter-balanced by the injury it will do to National Trade as a whole.

WE MUST SHARE OUR TRADE.

It is true that Germany, America, and the other industrial countries are manufacturing more than before. We had a long start upon them, but no policy of ours can prevent Germany working her coal and iron deposits, or America manufacturing the cotton products of her Southern States. Great Britain must make up her mind to share the trade of the world with her commercial rivals, for she can no longer monopolise it.

Our policy, therefore, must be to be economical with our wealth, and everything which increases the burdens of our industrial and industrious classes must be removed.

WHAT PROTECTION WILL DO.

If national economy and efficiency be our best policy, Protection is doubly condemned, for its immediate and most certain effects will be:

1. To enable the owners of land to increase rents:

2. To encourage the accumulation of capital in a few hands so that Trusts will control prices and conditions of labour: and thus

3. To limit the power of Trade Unions to improve the conditions of the wage-earners.

WE ARE MORE THAN FREE TRADERS.

We do not, however, regard Free Trade as in any way offering a solution to the problem of poverty. It is economically sound, and so we support it at the present crisis. It is right so far as it goes.

Free Trade has enabled us to accumulate National Wealth; a Labour Policy must now supplement Free Trade to enable us to distribute that wealth equitably.

WE MUST THROW OFF OUR BURDENS.

The burden of landlordism, the oppressive weight of mining rents and royalties, the unfair discrimination and the exactions of railway rates, not only handicap British industry in meeting foreign competition, but increase the difficulties of the wage-earners in making a living.

Therefore, in so far as the present Protectionist agitation draws attention to the burdens which British industry has to bear, we are thankful to Mr. Chamberlain. The Protectionist campaign should be made the occasion of the triumph of a Labour programme.

WE ATTACK, NOT ONLY DEFEND.

The Labour party demands better education, a more effective application of science to industry, better equipped Labour and Commercial State Departments, and, above all, graduated taxation of rents and of unearned and excessive incomes, so that the community may enjoy the wealth which it has created, and use that wealth to reduce the load of rates and taxes which is now oppressing legitimate industry. We also consider that in view of the high railway rates charged to British producers, the question of the nationalisation of railways should receive immediate attention.

These positive proposals we offer in reply to Mr. Chamberlain's appeals that we should retrace our steps and seek the assistance of a fiscal policy which we have already tried, and which neither protected our trade from loss nor guarded our people from starvation. We earnestly appeal to the workers of the country to support us in a campaign which will benefit the industrious classes by increasing national efficiency and securing a substantial reduction in the cost of production. Great Britain is not played out; she is bending under too heavy burdens. The British workman need never starve if his labour did not go to keep idle classes in luxury. Let our cry be: **"Increase Labour Representation in Parliament and decline to bear needless burdens."**

(*Signed*)

M. ABRAHAM, M.P.	C. FENWICK, M.P.
RICHARD BELL, M.P.	J. KEIR HARDIE, M.P.
JOHN BURNS, M.P.	ARTHUR HENDERSON, M.P.
HENRY BROADHURST, M.P.	D. J. SHACKLETON, M.P.
THOMAS BURT, M.P.	JOHN WILSON, M.P.
W. CROOKS, M.P.	

Parliamentary Committee of the Trade Union Congress:

F. CHANDLER, J.P., *Secretary, Amalgamated Carpenters and Joiners.*

EDWARD COWEY, *Miners' Federation.*

D. C. CUMMINGS, *Secretary, Boilermakers and Iron Shipbuilders.*

W. J. DAVIS, *Secretary, National Brassworkers' Union.*

A. H. GILL, J.P., *L.R.C. Candidate for Bolton, Amalgamated Cotton Spinners.*

D. HOLMES, J.P., *Northern Counties' Weavers.*

W. B. HORNIDGE, *Secretary, National Union Boot and Shoe Operatives.*

W. C. STEADMAN, *L.R.C. Candidate for Central Finsbury, Secretary Barge Builders.*

WILL THORNE, *L.R.C. Candidate for West Ham, Secretary, National Gasworkers and General Labourers.*

Management Committee of the General Federation of Trade Unions:

THOMAS ASHTON, *L.R.C. Candidate Oldham, Spinners' Cotton Operative Amalgamated Association.*

G. N. BARNES, *L.R.C. Candidate for Blackfriars Division of Glasgow, Secretary, Amalgamated Society of Engineers.*

JAMES CRINION, *Card and Blowing Room Operatives Amal. Association.*

J. MADDISON, *Secretary, Friendly Society of Ironfounders.*

THOMAS MALLALIEU, *Secretary, Amal. Society of Journeymen Felt Hatters.*

ISAAC MITCHELL, *Secretary, General Federation of Trade Unions.*

BEN TILLETT, *Secretary, Dock, Wharf, Riverside, and General Workers' Union.*

JOHN WARD, *L.R.C. Candidate for Stoke, Secretary, Navvies, Builders' Labourers and General Labourers' Union.*

Labour Representation Committee:

J. N. BELL, *Secretary, National Amalgamated Union of Labour.*

FREDERICK CROMPTON, *Amalgamated Society of Engineers.*

PETE CURRAN, *L.R.C. Candidate for Jarrow, National Gasworkers and General Labourers.*

CHARLES FREAKE, *President, National Union Boot and Shoe Operatives.*

ALLEN GEE, *Secretary, General Union of Weavers and Textile Workers.*

JOHN HODGE, *Chairman, L.R.C., L.R.C. Candidate for Gorton, Secretary, British Amal. Association of Steel Smelters.*

JAMES PARKER, *L.R.C. Candidate for Halifax.*

EDWARD R. PEASE, *Secretary, Fabian Society.*

J. SEXTON, *L.R.C. Candidate for North Shields, Secretary, National Union of Dock Labourers.*

BEN TURNER, *Secretary, Batley Weavers.*

A. WILKIE, *Secretary, Associated Shipwrights' Union.*

J. RAMSAY MACDONALD, *L.R.C. Candidate for Leicester, Secretary, L.R.C.*

LRC Policy Statement, 1906

31 Letter in 'The Times' from Fourteen Economists

One item in the conflict which particularly enraged tariff reformers was a letter appearing in *The Times* on 15 August 1903 signed by fourteen of the country's most distinguished economists. This clearly demonstrated their support for Free Trade, and provided the opposition to Chamberlain with authoritative academic backing. L. S. Amery, who as a young man at the time was an enthusiastic disciple of Chamberlain, retained his resentment at this pronouncement long enough to include an attack on these savants in his autobiography, published in 1953.

Professors of Economics and the Tariff Question.
To the Editor of the Times.

Sir,

We, the undersigned, beg leave to express our opinions of a more or less technical character connected with the fiscal proposals which now occupy the attention of the country.

One of the main objects aimed at in these proposals—the cultivation of friendly feelings between the United Kingdom and other parts of the Empire—is ardently desired by us; and we should not regard it as a fatal objection to a fiscal scheme adapted to this purpose that it was attended with a considerable sacrifice of material wealth. But the suggested means for attaining this desirable end do not seem to us advisable, first, because there would probably be incurred an immense and permanent sacrifice, not only of material, but also of higher goods; and, secondly, because the means suggested would be likely, in our judgement, to defeat rather than attain the end in view.

First, having regard to the prevalence of certain erroneous opinions, to which we advert below, we think that any system of preferential tariffs would most probably lead to the reintroduction of protection into the fiscal system of the United Kingdom. But a return to protection would, we hold, be detrimental to the material prosperity of this country, partly for reasons of the same kind as those which, as now universally admitted, justified the adoption of free trade—reasons which are now stronger than formerly, in consequence of the great proportion of food and raw materials imported from foreign countries, and the greater extent and complexity of our foreign trade. The evil would probably be a lasting one since experience shows that protection, when it has once taken root, is likely to extend beyond the limits at first assigned to it, and is very difficult to extirpate. There are also to be apprehended those evils other than material which protection brings in its train, the loss of purity in politics, the unfair advantage given to those who wield the powers of jobbery and corruption, unjust distribution of wealth, and the growth of "sinister interests".

Secondly, we apprehend that the suggested arrangements, far from promoting amity, may engender irritating controversies between the different members of the Empire. The growing sense of solidarity would be strained by an opposition of interests such as was experienced by our country under protection, and has been noticeable in the history of the United States and of other countries. Such an opposition of interests would be all the more disruptive in the case of the British Empire, as it is not held together by a central government.

Our convictions on this subject are opposed to certain popular opinions, with respect to which we offer the following observations.—

1. It is not true that an increase of imports involved the diminished employment of workmen in the importing country. The statement is universally rejected by those who have thought about the subject, and is completely refuted by experience.

2. It is very improbable that a tax on food imported into the United Kingdom would result in an equivalent—or more than equivalent—rise in wages. The result which may be anticipated as a direct consequence of the tax is a lowering of the real remuneration of labour.

3. The injury which the British consumer would receive from an import tax on wheat might be slightly reduced in the possible,

K

but under existing circumstances very improbable, event of a small proportion of the burden being thrown permanently on the foreign producer.

4. To the statement that a tax on food will raise the price of food, it is not a valid reply that this result may possibly in fact not follow. When we say that an import duty raises price, we mean, of course, unless its effect is overborne by other causes operating at the same time in the other direction. Or, in other words, we mean that in consequence of the import duty the price is generally higher by the amount of the duty than it would have been if other things had remained the same.

5. It seems to us impossible to devise any tariff regulation which shall at once expand the wheat-growing areas in the Colonies, encourage agriculture in the United Kingdom, and at the same time not injure the British consumer.

6. The suggestion that the public, though clearly damnified by an impost, may yet obtain a full equivalent from its yield is incorrect, because it leaves out of account the interference with the free circulation of goods, the detriment incidental to diverting industry from the course which it would otherwise have taken, and the circumstance that, in the case of a tax on foreign wheat— English and Colonial wheat being free—while the consumer would have to pay the whole or nearly the whole tax on all the wheat, the Government would get the tax only on foreign wheat.

7. In general, those who lightly undertake to reorganise the supply of food and otherwise divert the course of industry do not adequately realise what a burden of proof rests on the politician who, leaving the plain rule of taxation for the sake of revenue only, seeks to attain ulterior objects by manipulating tariffs.

C. F. BASTABLE (Professor of Political Economy at the University of Dublin.)

A. L. BOWLEY (appointed Teacher of Statistics in the University of London at the London School of Economics.)

EDWIN CANNAN (appointed Teacher of Economic Theory

in the University of London at the London School of Economics.)

LEONARD COURTNEY (formerly Professor of Political Economy at University College, London.)

F. Y. EDGEWORTH (Professor of Political Economy at the University of Oxford.)

E. C. K. GONNER (Professor of Economic Science at the University of Liverpool.)

ALFRED MARSHALL (Professor of Political Economy at the University of Cambridge.)

J. S. NICHOLSON (Professor of Political Economy at the University of Edinburgh.)

L. R. PHELPS (Editor of the *Economic Review*.)

A. PIGOU (Jevons Memorial Lecturer at University College, London.)

C. P. SANGER (Lecturer in Political Economy at University College.)

W. R. SCOTT (Lecturer in Political Economy at the University of St. Andrews.)

W. SMART (Professor of Political Economy at the University of Glasgow.)

ARMITAGE SMITH (Lecturer in Political Economy at the Birkbeck College, Recognised Teacher of the University of London in Economics.)

The Times, 15 August 1903

32 Punch cartoon
Much of the political conflict of 1903–6 over commercial policy, however, did not pretend to this high intellectual plane. A cartoon in *Punch*, for example, shows Balfour and Chamberlain in discussion over the bogeyman of foreign competition.

AN EYE FOR EFFECT.

Arthur. "AIN'T YOU MADE 'IM TOO 'ORRIBLE?"
Joe. "NO FEAR! YOU *CAN'T* MAKE 'EM TOO 'ORRIBLE!"

33 and 34 Tariff Reform Posters
These are two posters produced by the Tariff Reformers for the general election of 1906, and show how the simplified version of their arguments were given publicity.

35 LRC Poster (overleaf)
To complement the previous pair, this poster is one of a series of well-designed bills produced by the LRC for the 1906 general election. The monocled figure wearing an orchid in the buttonhole is Chamberlain, and the poster gives a graphic illustration of the arguments put forward in the manifesto cited as No 30 here.

36 The Hungry Forties, or Life under the Bread Tax
The value of the use—or perhaps more accurately the mis-use—of historical arguments was fully appreciated during the Tariff Reform crisis of 1903–6. The Free Traders in particular resorted to a great deal of historical exposition to validate their position. In particular, they contrived to imply that everything had been dark and unpleasant in the bad old days before the Corn Laws were repealed, whereas the coming of Free Trade had brought immense improvement. The kind of propaganda involved here is well illustrated by these passages from a book produced with help from Cobden's family in 1904.

DAVID MILES, LABOURER, HEYSHOTT VILLAGE.

"Ay, I reklects the early forties afore the Corn Laws wor repealed. 'Taters was what folks lived on then, an' the Tories' ud 'ave it that a red 'errin' and a 'tater wor good enuff for any workin'-man. When I wor just on twelve the 'taters failed, an' never shall I forgit 'ow the folks went a-wanderin' about, peerin' at the 'taters, and tryin' to find out what wor wrong wi' 'em. It wor awful bad for the low class; many on 'em were nigh starvin'. If 'ee complained to the masters, they on'y said, quite indiff'rent, ' 'Ee can go; we don't want 'ee.' An' if 'ee went to the vestry, which they wor every blessed one on 'em farmers, and said as 'ow

'ee wanted work, they'd ask, 'Who've 'ee bin a-workin' for?' an' when 'ee answered, 'Mr. So-an'-so,' up the farmer 'd get and declare 'ee was dissatisfied, and then ne'er a one 'ud have anythin' more to do with 'ee. 'Twas ne'er a bit o' good leavin' the parish; they'd ask 'ee where did 'ee be come from, and when 'ee said, 'Heyshott,' they'd say as 'ow they didn't want no furriners, and that there ud be the end o't. It worn't no manner o' good a-tryin' to raise yerself, 'ee wor just a slave, and that's the truth. Them what cudn't get work 'ad to go on the parish or starve. Nowadays there's a many what 'a'n't got no manner o' notion what Protection is and think they'd like to 'ave a taste o't, but we old 'uns, we knows—lor' bless 'ee! we knows. Folks call 'em the good old times; that's just their ignorance; I call 'em the bad old times I do, when a few got fat and 'unnerds starved. If Mr. Cobden 'adn't got 'em Corn Laws repealed there'd 'ave bin a reg'lar Civil War in this yer country years ago. Folks used to put up a little 'ill o' taters for the winter, not two rods from their winders, but people 'ud come by night and steal 'em. A 'ungry belly makes a man desprit. They'd steal a'most anything, even bees and brocli from the garden. When a man 'ad a large fa'am'ly, they were pretty nigh starvin' mostly; as for meat, a look in at the butcher's shop was all theeir share o' that. The 'oomen ud cut off the black crust from the loafs and put it in the teapot and pour water on it instid o' tea; it looked pretty much the same colour, d'ye see; or else they'd beg the tea-leaves from the big houses.

"Ten hours a day is what we worked, a-threshin' corn in the barn. 'Twas hard, wearin' work; two o' us 'ud do it together; and 'ee 'ad to keep in turn, I can tell 'ee, or 'ee got a taste o' your neighbour's flail on the side o' yer face; many a one's got a black eye for threshin' out o' turn. Them that cudn't get work 'ud sometimes fire the barn. I got a job once six an' a 'alf mile away, and that seemed a fair step, I can tell 'ee, when I come 'ome tired of an evenin'; but I used to pass a 'ooman on the way what 'ad to dig up turmuts wid white frost on 'em, and I wouldn't 'a 'ad 'er job, bless 'ee, for a pound a week, that I wouldn't.

'Oomen used to 'ave to go a-weedin' in the corn in them days.

"When Mr. Cobden come 'ere Tiller and fifteen more wor a-breakin' stones on the road for eightpence a day, that's just all they cud get; but Mr. Cobden 'e altered all that. I and some other youngsters 'ud meet 'im sometimes when we wor a-goin' to school; 'e didn't take much notice o' we; 'e allus seemed in a deep study. I've thought since that 'e wor just a-plannin' some good for 'is fellow-creatures. I reklects when I an' my brother wor a-goin' to school 'ow we'd see the big loaf for Free Trade and the small loaf for Protection stuck up in one o' the winders, and my brother 'e sez, 'Well,' he sez, 'the big loaf's the best.' "

Our next letter is from Mr. Wm. Prestidge, of 28, Manor Road, Bishopston, Bristol:—

"I was born in the parish of Meriden, near Coventry, Warwickshire, 76 years ago, and can well remember those 'good old times,' falsely so called, as they were anything but good times to my dear father and mother and us 5 children. His wages were but 9/- per week, with 2 pence per day that I got for frightening the crows off a farmer's wheat, making another 11d. per week to keep seven of us, and father had to pay 6 pounds per year out of that for his house to live in, so you may guess how we lived with the 4-lb. loaf at 11½d., tea from 5 to 8 shillings per lb., and vile sugar at 9 pence per lb. Then meat—mutton, beef, and poultry—I don't know how they were sold—we could only see those things. One ounce of tea and a pound of bacon a week, with a dish or two of swedes thrown in, if we could get them, as the potatoes were a great failure after the disease set in, which has continued more or less ever since, and was the cause of thousands of deaths in Ireland. And from frightening the crows off the farmer's wheat, when I got a bit older I used to help father thrash out the corn, with two heavy sticks swinging over my head all day, on barley and wheat bread and small beer, in the farmer's barn; and we used to have 'tea-kettle broth' for breakfast. What would the young people think of such a breakfast as that to-day? I never had a day's schooling in my life, but was always brought up to behave myself lowly and reverently to all my betters. My dear father died at 43 years of age through hard work, bad living, and other terrible hardships; an now Joseph Chamberlain wants to bring us back to those good old times again with his Fiscal Policy and Protection." *The Hungry Forties, or Life under the Bread Tax*, with an Introduction by Mrs Cobden Unwin, London, 1904

37 Stanley Baldwin   Speeches at Plymouth and Swansea

Bonar Law, a supporter of Chamberlain's Tariff Reform policies, became prime minister in October 1922. During the general election of the following month, to the dismay of many of his fellow tariff-reformers, he promised that he would not introduce protection without an express mandate from the people, for which he was not then asking. In May 1923 he was forced to resign, to die a few months later, and Baldwin took his place. Baldwin, himself a protégé of Bonar Law, was likewise a believer in tariffs; it was no coincidence that both men had close ties with the iron industry, as Chamberlain himself had, for that was one industry which was very obviously affected by the growth of foreign competition. Baldwin determined to try to introduce Tariff Reform only a few months after he had become premier. It is by no means certain that this step was taken solely on grounds of economic policy. Political factors may also have counted. It has been suggested that Baldwin wished to use Tariff Reform to bring back into the fold Austen Chamberlain and his colleagues from the old Lloyd George coalition who had refused to join Bonar Law in breaking with Lloyd George. Austen Chamberlain had inherited his father's Tariff Reform views, so the lure might be effective. An alternative explanation was Baldwin's desire to forestall any attempt by Lloyd George to occupy the Tariff Reform platform. Whatever the real reason or reasons may have been Baldwin's gamble failed to pay off in the election of 1923. His party was unprepared, and Free Trade sentiment still strong. The following passages are taken from the speech in which Baldwin took the plunge, and one of the follow-up speeches made a few days later.

(i) *Baldwin at Plymouth, 25 October 1923*

He promised that the Government would proceed in the autumn session to take whatever legislative steps may be necessary in connexion with any of the measures to help unemployment which they had proposed, and if any particular case of hardship could be made out he would have no hesitation in asking the Chancellor of the Exchequer to safeguard certain industries.

The Prime Minister described the unemployment problem as the crucial problem of our country, but said he could not fight it without weapons. He referred to Mr. Bonar Law's pledge that there should be no fundamental change in the fiscal arrangements of the country. "That pledge binds me," he said, "and in this Parliament there will be no fundamental change. I take those words strictly. I am not the man to play with a pledge, but I cannot see myself that any slight extension or adaptation of principles hitherto sanctioned in the Legislature are breaches of that pledge, but any time I am challenged I am always willing to take a verdict."

Then came a dramatic declaration which roused the meeting to great enthusiasm. "I have for myself", he said, "come to the conclusion that, having regard to the situation of our country, if we go pottering about as we are we shall have grave unemployment with us to the end of time. I have come to the conclusion that the only way of fighting this subject is by protecting the home market." "Good old Baldwin" came cries, and loud and long cheering followed. . . . *The Times*, 26 October 1923

(ii) *Baldwin at Swansea, 30 October 1923*

The dream of universal Free Trade was but a dream, and cannot be dreamed today. Foreign countries have not followed us. Our own Dominions have not followed us. They have preferred to preserve their own market and to preserve their own agriculture as a background. We are the one exception. We have believed in a splendid isolation at home even when that isolation is accompanied by phenomenal unemployment. That cannot be witnessed today in any industrial country in the world. Ideals require examination. Universal Free Trade is an ideal. It may or may not be a good thing, but it is not in the region of practical politics (hear, hear)—and to those who do not regard a fiscal system as made for man, but who regard man as made for a fiscal system—and that system Free Trade—I would say to them there will be far more chance of approaching their ideal by helping to approximate the system of this country to that of every other country, and when that is done you may quite conceivably have a far more equitable transport of goods from one country to another—less impeded by tariffs than you have ever had before.

For with tariffs, as with armaments, an unarmed nation will never make an armed nation disarm. But when you have nations of comparatively equal strength you may achieve results ... with tariffs, when all can speak on an equality, and no one is defenceless, you then may have an opportunity of driving your bargains and of getting freer trade than you have ever had before. ... *The Times*, 31 October 1923

38 H. H. Asquith   Speech at Dewsbury
Once again the bringing of the tariff issue into the limelight proved a godsend to a sadly divided Liberal party. Liberal unity had been broken by the government crisis at the end of 1916 which had seen Asquith lose the premiership to Lloyd George. However, in 1923 both men were willing to fight in defence of Free Trade, despite their distrust of each other. The tariff proposals at the time had some obvious weaknesses, and in this passage from a speech at Dewsbury on 5 November 1923 Asquith points some of them out.

... let me dispose once and for all on the threshold of this controversy of the absurd fiction that those of us who always have been, and still are, convinced and unrepentant Free Traders, are so in deference to a kind of superstitious idolatry ... I have always based my advocacy of Free Trade, not upon abstractions, not upon dogmas, not upon the authority of Cobden and Bright, least of all upon Utopian dreams of a beneficent ideal of universal Free Trade. I have based the cause always, and exclusively, upon the hard concrete facts of the actual economic conditions and requirements of Great Britain. (Cheers.) It is possible—indeed we know it to be the fact—that after the repeal of the Corn Laws there were enthusiasts who not only hoped but believed that all the world was going to follow our example. For the last sixty years I know of no Free Trader in this island who has rested his case upon any such illusion. The question with the British Free Trader has always been—What is the best policy for Great Britain in view of the actual conditions of the world? (Cheers.) ... An analysis has been made for me of the proportion of the total unemployment which belongs to industries that could be helped by the new tariff. The total of unemployed is roughly 1,340,000. The number of those who belong to the trades in question is not greater than 140,000—that is to say about 10.4 per cent. of the whole. . . . The trades which are the most depressed, to which the great majority of the unemployed belong —shipbuilding, engineering, cotton and some parts of the woollen industry, not to mention transportation and distribution— are of a kind that no tariff would help. . . . *The Times*, 6 November 1923

39 David Lloyd George   Speech in London

A speech by Lloyd George in London on 21 November 1923 was part of the same campaign, and illustrates the specious and slick arguments which could readily be assembled by the Welsh wizard.

Once again in the general election of December 1923 the defence of Free Trade proved successful, though in this instance the political beneficiary was not the ailing Liberal party. The immediate result of Baldwin's rash decision was the formation of the first Labour government.

We were dependent for four-fifths of our supplies upon the foreigner. It was impossible to make this small country self-contained. Foreign trade was vital to its very existence. We should starve without it.

He challenged anyone to deny that this country "Ruined by free trade", was the greatest exporter of the produce of its factories of any country in the world in proportion to its output. Take the leading industries of this country—cotton, wool, shipping, machinery, iron and steel. We beat every country in the world in the export of our own manufactures of these goods. . . . What was the good of saying that this country was being ruined by free imports? Free imports were keeping it alive. (Cheers.) Free trade had an advantage in neutral markets over tariffs. Why? A large buyer had always the advantage of the customer when he came to sell. We were the greatest buyers in the world, and therefore the greatest sellers. We went to countries who bought, and when they bought we sold. It had taken 80 years to adapt our commerce to one fiscal system. Tariff reformers now said, "Give up the system that has made you, given you the best credit in Europe, the best wages in Europe, made you the greatest exporter of manufactured goods in the world, given you the greatest shipping the world had ever seen—give it up, start another system, adapt yourselves to that, and do it to cure unemployment". It was lunacy. . . . (Cheers.) *The Times*, 22 November 1923

40 Ramsay MacDonald Speech at Victoria

The Labour Party had played its part in this electoral battle, joining the Liberals in their attacks on Baldwin's policy of Tariff Reform, but claiming that Labour alone possessed a positive alternative policy, and was now the natural choice to succeed the Conservatives as a governing party.

Here is a short passage from a speech delivered at Victoria on 2 November 1923 by Ramsay MacDonald, soon to take office as Labour's first premier. If the intellectual content of the previous passage from Lloyd George is not impressive, the

Labour leader's grasp of economic argument is no greater, and the speech illustrated that the woolliness in MacDonald's oratory, which increased alarmingly in future years, was already present when he took office for the first time.

———

Protection was not a cure, it was a diversion—a magnificent method of side-tracking a serious movement. When the cry of Protection was last raised, it was fought on negative issues. But the fight now would be, not Protection versus Free Trade, but Protection versus the Labour policy. (Cheers.) Supposing we had Protection, we should still have unemployment, land monopoly, starvation in education, and all the other social problems for the solution of which the Labour movement stood and would continue to stand despite the red herrings drawn across its path. (Cheers.)

There was not a single nation in the world which was running its industry under Protection that had not got the problem of the normal unemployed. Protection never had solved that, and never would. . . . To the cry, "Protect our own markets", Labour replied, "Develop our own country". They were going to work their own country for all it was worth, to bring human labour into touch with God's natural endowments, so that the land would blossom like the rose and have houses and firesides where there would be happiness and glorious aspirations. (Cheers.) *The Times*, 2 November 1923

———

PART FIVE

The Fall of Free Trade

So far all the attacks on Free Trade had foundered on the rock-like belief that Free Trade had worked for Britain; a natural *post hoc propter hoc* assumption tied up the growth of British wealth with the commercial policy under which it had come about. The connection seemed so self-evident that for most people the pragmatic justification of Free Trade was sufficient. This touching faith was destroyed in the great depression of 1929–31. It was not so much that most people understood what exactly had gone wrong, for they did not, but rather that faith in old methods was shaken by what seemed their terrible failure in these years, and the urgent necessity to try something new to make good the damage.

From Chamberlain's 1903 crusade on, Tariff Reform had always had powerful advocates within the Conservative party, while the more sophisticated economic theorists of the generation of John Maynard Keynes (1883–1946) were less united and certain in their defence of Free Trade.

The deepening crisis brought about the fall of the second Labour government in August 1931 and its replacement by a National government whose mission was to introduce emergency measures to deal with the deteriorating financial position of the country. In this new government the Conservatives were in a strong position, though MacDonald remained prime minister. The National government included some Free Traders—men like Philip Snowden (1864–1937), who had twice demonstrated his orthodoxy as Labour Chancellor of the Exchequer, and Sir Herbert Samuel (1870–1963), who had led the Liberal party into the National government. Even these men, however, were willing in 1931 to swallow temporary emergency measures that flouted the principles of Free Trade: the two Acts mainly concerned here were an Abnormal Importations Act and a Horticultural Products Act, both clearly examples of protection. Even Winston Churchill was now brought to see that the old Free Trade shibboleths must be sacrificed to the present emergency.

The temporary emergency measures and the formation of the National government did not prevent the devaluation of the pound, but the general election of October 1931 confirmed the National government in office, conferring on it an enormous majority in which the Conservative element was by far the biggest. The Tariff Reformers were now emboldened to replace the temporary Acts of 1931 by a more permanent and systematic abandonment of Free Trade, and this victory was consummated in 1932, the government shedding its Free Traders in the process (41, 42). The long series of combats were over, and Free Trade abandoned.

The interest of these months is not just political, for there were significant developments in financial and economic theories. The Macmillan Committee on Finance and Industry, appointed in November 1929, reported in June 1931. Its investigations show how techniques of enquiry had developed beyond the standard set by the Import Duties Committee of 1840 (8). The main Report of this important Committee was cautious, and much of the interest of its work lies in the evidence taken and in the various addenda added to the main Report. Keynes drafted the most influential of these, which was signed by six of the Committee's fourteen members (43). The economic theorists were not, however, speaking with one voice, as was made clear by an addendum by Professor T. E. Gregory (44). It is notable, however, that in all these theoretical discussions the question of Free Trade versus Protection no longer occupies the centre of the stage. Whether or not tariffs or quota regulations should be employed is no longer the cardinal question, but is at best a tactical expedient. Few people now believed that government could avoid intervening in the economic life of the state, though the degree and manner of that intervention remained matters of argument. Little more than lip service was to be paid in future to Cobdenite ideas. The innovations of 1931–2 marked the close of an era.

This selection ends with a polemical essay by Keynes, composed during this crisis, in piquant contrast to the passage from *The Wealth of Nations* with which we began. In it Keynes accepts that tariffs are a useful device in present circumstances. A few months after it was published the second Labour government gave way to the National government, which abolished Free Trade in a way that made Keynes's last sentence remarkably prophetic (45).

41 Neville Chamberlain   Speech in Parliament

The Chancellor of the Exchequer under whom Britain finally abandoned Free Trade was Neville Chamberlain (1869–1940), the younger son of the Tariff Reformer Joseph Chamberlain. Backed by an overwhelming majority after the general election of 1931, the cabinet members who were Protectionists could afford to lose their Free Trade colleagues like Snowden and Samuel, who mourned the passing of old principles in vain. The following passage is taken from Neville Chamberlain's speech to the House of Commons in Committee on 4 February 1932, in which he outlined the basis of the government's long-term commercial policy.

... before I come to the details of the Government's intended Measures, I think perhaps it would be convenient if I were to try to give to the Committee a very brief summary of the objects at which we are aiming, in order that they may perhaps get a better picture of the general scope and range of our intentions. First of all, we desire to correct the balance of payments by diminishing our imports and stimulating our exports. Then we desire to fortify the finances of the country by raising fresh revenue by methods which will put no undue burden upon any section of the community. We wish to effect an insurance against a rise in the cost of living which might easily follow upon an unchecked depreciation of our currency. We propose, by a system of moderate Protection, scientifically adjusted to the needs of industry and agriculture, to transfer to our own factories and our own fields work which is now done elsewhere, and thereby decrease unemployment in the only satisfactory way in which it can be diminished.

We hope by the judicious use of this system of Protection to enable and to encourage our people to render their methods of production and distribution more efficient. We mean also to use it for negotiations with foreign countries which have not hitherto paid very much attention to our suggestions, and, at the same time, we think it prudent to arm ourselves with an instrument which shall at least be as effective as those which may be used to discriminate against us in foreign markets. Last, but not least, we are going to take the opportunity of offering advantages to the countries of the Empire in return for the advantages which they now give, or in the near future may be disposed to give, to us. In that summary, under seven heads, we believe that we have framed a policy which will bring new hope and new heart to this country, and will lay the foundations of a new spirit of unity and co-operation throughout the Empire.

The Bill which will embody these proposals will, of course, not be available to the Committee this afternoon. It cannot be introduced until the Committee has passed the Ways and Means Resolutions, of which there are four. The text of these Resolutions will be available as soon as I sit down, and in moving the first of them I understand that it is agreed to be for the convenience of the Committee that a general discussion shall take place ranging over all the four Resolutions, but they will, of course, be voted upon separately when the Debate concludes.

The basis of our proposals is what we call a general *ad valorem* duty of 10 per cent. upon all imports into this country, with certain exceptions to which I shall allude a little later. The purposes of that general duty are two-fold. We desire to raise by it a substantial contribution to the Revenue, and we desire also to put a general brake upon the total of the imports coming in here.

Of course, if our sole object were the reduction of imports, we might achieve that purpose by a different method. We could take certain particular items and exclude them altogether. That would be a method which would bring about the greatest possible disturbance of trade, and in introducing a fundamental change of this character we naturally desire to do it with as little dislocation of existing arrangements as may be found necessary. There are, however, certain exceptions to that general duty. Wherever there is an existing duty the article so dutiable will not be subject to the 10 per cent., and that applies equally to such duties as those on tobacco, or sugar, or coffee, to the so-called McKenna Duties, to the Safeguarding Duties, the key industry duties, and also to the duties under the two Acts which I mentioned before, the Abnormal Importations and the Horticultural Products Acts until the duties under those Acts expire, when they will be replaced by the flat rate duty unless some other arrangement is made, of which I shall make mention again directly.

There is also a free list of no great length which will be included in a Schedule to the Bill. I do not propose this afternoon to go through the free list. It is not necessary, for the purpose of the Resolutions, but I may give some indication to the Committee, and mention one or two of the most important items which are included in it. In the free list will appear wheat in grain. The Committee is aware that it is the intention of the Government to deal with the importation of wheat by means of a quota system. There is also meat, which includes bacon, one of the staple foods of the people, and fresh fish of British taking, which I am advised includes also those members of the mollusca and crustacea which form such a desirable and ornamental addition to our dinner table. There will also be found in the free list the raw materials of the two great textile industries, raw cotton and raw wool. Then there is tea, and I think I ought to tell the Committee that tea is put into the free list of this Bill because it is considered to be more convenient to deal with tea in conjunction with other beverages, such as coffee and cocoa, in the ordinary course of the Budget. I must also warn the Committee that they must not assume that tea is going to be or is not going to be taxed in the next Budget, because that is a subject upon which I must reserve a doctor's mandate until Budget day comes.

I now pass to the superstructure which it is proposed to build upon the general *ad valorem* duties. That superstructure takes the form of additional duties which may be imposed upon non-essential articles. When I speak of non-essential articles, I mean either articles of luxury which are not essential to the individual, or articles which are not essential to the nation, in the sense that they either can be now or could be very shortly produced at home in substantial and sufficient quantity. We do not propose to specify these additional duties in the Bill; we propose that these duties may be imposed by Order of the Treasury after consultation with the appropriate Department, which will be the Board of Trade or the Ministry of Agriculture, or other Department concerned.

But the Treasury will not take the initiative in this matter. It would be extremely undesirable to put the selection of articles to be made dutiable, or the rates of duty to be levied, into the discretion of a single Minister. I am quite sure that his life would be very soon made intolerable by the demands which would be addressed to him, but, in addition to that, it might be thought that the decisions of such a Minister had been influenced by political considerations. Accordingly, it is proposed to set up an independent advisory committee consisting of a chairman and not less than two or more than five other members. This committee will be expected to give its whole time to its duties, and will be paid a salary which will be proportionate to the standing which we shall require of the members and to the sort of judicial attitude that we shall expect of them. It will be their function to consider the circumstances of those non-essential articles which are already subject to the duty of 10 per cent., and to recommend whether additional duties shall be placed on them;

and, in making their recommendations, they will be instructed to have regard to the advisability in the national interest of restricting imports into the United Kingdom, and they must also consider the general interests of trade and industry, including the interests of the trades which are consumers as well as those which are producers of goods. The duties which they may recommend may be either ad valorem or specific; they may be permanent, or they may be temporary, or they may be seasonal; and in certain cases the Committee will also have the power of recommending that drawbacks shall be applied.

One of their first tasks will be to consider what is to happen to the duties now imposed under the two Acts to which I have already made more than one allusion, and it will be seen that they will have full power to recommend either that those duties shall be continued as they are, or that they shall be reduced, it may be by degrees, or that they shall be replaced by the flat-rate duty, or that they shall disappear altogether. Complete freedom is left to the committee to make whatever recommendations they think are in the best interests of industry as a whole. On the receipt of a recommendation from this committee, the Treasury will be empowered to make Orders directing that a duty may be imposed upon the article specified, at a rate not exceeding the rate which has been recommended by the committee. *Parliamentary Debates*, 5th Series, Commons, Vol 261, col 287-90

42 House of Commons   Debate on Tariff Reform and Free Trade

This passage records the result of the prolonged debate in Committee on the government's proposals. A small but determined opposition, made up of Labour members and some inveterate Liberal Free Traders, resisted to the last. These votes were taken in the House of Commons on 9 February 1932.

Question put,
"That there shall, subject as hereinafter provided, be charged

as from the first day of March, nineteen hundred and thirty-two, on all goods imported into the United Kingdom a duty of customs equal to ten per cent. of the value of the goods;

Provided that the duty aforesaid shall not be charged on the following goods, that is to say,—

(*a*) goods for the time being chargeable with any other duty of customs (not being a duty chargeable by or under any Act of the present Session for giving effect to this and any other Resolution), but not including composite goods except as may be provided by the Act aforesaid; or

(*b*) goods of any class or description which may be exempted by the Act aforesaid from the duty charged by this Resolution."

The Committee divided: Ayes, 452; Noes, 76.

ADDITIONAL CUSTOMS DUTIES.

Motion made, and Question put,
"That—

(i) there shall be charged, in accordance with the provisions of this Resolution, on the importation into the United Kingdom of any goods to which this Resolution applies such duties of customs as are hereinafter provided:

(ii) the goods to which this Resolution shall apply shall be goods of any class or description which—

(*a*) are liable to any general ad valorem customs duty which may be charged by any Act of the present Session for giving effect to this and any other Resolution; and

(*b*) appear to the Committee to be constituted for the purpose of giving advice and assistance to the Treasury in connection with the discharge by the Treasury of any of their functions under the aforesaid Act, to be either articles of luxury or articles of a kind which are being produced or are likely within a reasonable time to be produced in the United Kingdom in quantities which are substantial in relation to United Kingdom consumption; and

(*c*) are the subject of a recommendation by the Committee

aforesaid to the Treasury to the effect that an additional duty of customs should be charged thereon;

(iii) the Treasury, after receiving such a recommendation as aforesaid, may by order direct that an additional duty of customs shall be charged on all or any of the goods specified in the recommendation at a rate not exceeding the rate specified in the recommendation;

(iv) Any additional duties, according as may be directed by the order aforesaid, may be charged—

(*a*) by reference to value, to weight, to measurement, or to quantity;

(*b*) for any period or periods, whether continuous or not, or without any limit of period;

(*c*) at different rates for different periods or parts of periods."—[*Mr. Chamberlain.*]

The Committee proceeded to a Division.

Sir CHARLES OMAN (*seated and covered*): On a point of Order. On the analogy of the great English game, would it not be possible now for the Government to declare at 452, and put in the Opposition for a second, a third, and a fourth innings, which would enable us to save a good deal of time?

The Committee divided: Ayes, 430; Noes, 73.

Customs Duties in Respect of Foreign Discrimination.

Motion made, and Question put,

"That—

(i) there shall in addition to any other duties of customs be charged, in accordance with the provisions of this Resolution, on the importation into the United Kingdom of any goods to which this Resolution applies, such duties of customs as are hereinafter mentioned;

(ii) the goods to which this Resolution shall apply shall be goods of any class or description to which the Board of Trade may by order apply the provisions for giving effect to this Resolution contained in any Act of the present Session, as being goods produced or manufactured in any foreign country which discriminates in respect of the importation into that country of goods produced or manufactured in the United Kingdom (including the Isle of Man), the Channel Islands, any colony or any territory which is under His Majesty's protection or in respect of which a mandate is being exercised by the Government of the United Kingdom, as against the United Kingdom (including the Isle of Man), the Channel Islands, that colony or that territory;

(iii) The duties to be charged by virtue of any such order as aforesaid in respect of any goods—

(a) shall be such duties as may be specified in the order not exceeding one hundred per cent. of the value of the goods; and

(b) may be charged by reference to value, to weight, to measurement, or to quantity, as may be provided in the order."—[*Mr. N. Chamberlain.*]

The Committee divided: Ayes, 421; Noes, 68.

Parliamentary Debates, 5th Series, Commons, Vol 261, col 807–12.

43 J. M. Keynes   Addendum to Report of the Macmillan Committee

J. M. Keynes drafted the first and most influential addendum to the Report of the Macmillan Committee. It was signed by five other members, including the two Labour men on the Committee, Ernest Bevin and Thomas Allen. In the passage quoted here, Keynes argues in favour of measures incompatible with continued Free Trade. It is noticeable, though, that these measures are put forward primarily as an alternative to devaluation and are far from occupying the centre of the argument. We are in any event far from the moral fervour of a Cobden or a Bright, and instead brought face to face with practical necessity.

(b)   *Tariffs plus Bounties.*

34. Precisely the same effects as those produced by a devaluation of sterling by a given percentage could be brought about by a tariff of the same percentage on all imports together with an equal subsidy on all exports, except that this measure *would leave*

sterling international obligations unchanged in terms of gold. This proposal would avoid the injury to the national credit and to our receipts from foreign loans fixed in terms of sterling which would ensue on devaluation.

35. Under existing commercial treaties, however, there would be practical difficulties in the way of a direct subsidy to exports. Nevertheless, various plans might be propounded for combining some form of restriction of imports with granting sundry indirect advantages to the export industries, which would represent an approximation to the above scheme. We consider that a plan of this kind would be so immeasurably preferable to devaluation, that it is foolish even to discuss the latter while the former remains untried.

36. It is worth while to remark that, if the level of domestic money-incomes is such that our international equilibrium would be restored by a reduction of money-incomes or by the devaluation of sterling, then it follows that, failing the adoption of one or other of these two expedients, the optimum distribution of the national resources between different uses will result, not from Free Trade, but from as near an approximation as is practicable to a *Tariff plus Bounties* measure on the above lines.

37. The avowed object of such a measure as this would be to reduce the value of a given money-income; though the cost of living might be expected to rise by only a fraction of the percentage rate of duty. Its advantages would be two. In the first place it would be fair; for every description of money-income would be affected equally. In the second place, it would involve no disturbance to confidence and no breach of understanding with our foreign creditors. . . .

II.—CONTROL OF IMPORTS AND AIDS TO EXPORTS.

39. Proposals under this heading raise political and social issues which extend far beyond the necessities of the present emergency. A specific may be appropriate to a particular situation, and yet be rejected in obedience to wider considerations more extended in time. We do not propose to attempt any such

summing up of the final balance of advantage and disadvantage, having regard to all the relevant factors, as would be needed to justify a definite recommendation. We shall confine ourselves, therefore, to considering briefly the uses of tariffs or Import Boards, etc., and subsidies on articles of foreign trade regarded as an expedient to meet a situation in which a country has a large unemployed surplus of labour and of plant which it is unable to bring into use in the conditions imposed on it by its economic relations, arising out of relative rates of interest and money-costs, with the rest of the world.

40. The fundamental argument for unrestricted Free Trade does not apply without qualification to an economic system which is neither in equilibrium nor in sight of equilibrium. For if a country's productive resources are normally fully employed, a tariff cannot increase output, but can only divert production from one direction into another, whilst there is a general presumption that the natural direction for the employment of resources, which they can reach on their merits and without being given special advantages at the expense of others, will yield a superior national dividend. But if this condition of full employment is neither fulfilled nor likely to be fulfilled for some time, then the position is totally different, since a tariff may bring about a net increase of production and not merely a diversion.

41. It appears to us, therefore, that, if imports were to be controlled, whether by a tariff with compensation for exports, or by Import Boards, or in some other way and home-produced goods substituted for them, there is a presumption, so long as present circumstances last, that this would mean a net increase of employment and of national productivity. Into the rate of the tariff and the classes of the articles affected we do not enter.

42. The arguments most commonly adduced on the other side—apart from long-period considerations which we are not pretending to discuss—are the following:—

(i) It is said that the restriction of certain kinds of imports would curtail foreign buying power and so diminish the market for our exports. This would be true if we were to use our improved balance of trade to import gold and the consequent loss of gold by the rest of the world had the effect of causing a contraction of total credit. But if we make use of our improved balance of trade to expand investment at home with the result of increasing our imports of food and raw materials (an expansion which would have led to a *loss* of gold by us if we had attempted it without a contemporaneous restriction of imports) or to increase our foreign lending, then it need have no adverse effect on the market for our exports.

(ii) It is said that a restriction of imports would tend to increase the cost of production of our exports. This is a question of degree depending on the kind of restriction imposed. Clearly a substantial tax on imported raw materials without a rebate for exports would have a seriously adverse effect on exports. At the other extreme, it is not evident that a tax on the importation of luxury motor cars or an Import Board for pig products would have any appreciable consequences of this kind. It is easy to conceive both of a tariff, accompanied by appropriate rebates, and of Import Boards the effect of which on the cost of exports would be small compared with that of other factors. Nor is there any reason to suppose that the effect on exports need be commensurate with the effect on imports.

Nevertheless, even if these measures were so devised as to impose only a small handicap on our exports, this would be *pro tanto* an objection. The logical course, in our opinion, would be to find ways of giving equivalent advantages to the export industries. For much of the argument in favour of a restriction of imports applies equally to a subsidy to exports. A direct subsidy would be open to various practical objections. But it would not be difficult to find other ways of giving back to the export industries advantages at least equal in amount to the comparatively small disadvantages which would be imposed on them by those effects of restricting imports by a tariff or otherwise which would be individually too small and incalculable to be dealt with by means of a rebate.

(iii) The third objection, which is most commonly heard,

relates to the effect on the cost of living of the working classes. The force of this objection depends partly on the character of the tariff or other measures in view, and partly on a comparison with the effect on the cost of living of those measures to which the tariff is offered as an alternative.

For example, a given amount of revenue raised by taxing manufactured imports would probably increase the cost of living less than if it were raised by taxes on tea, sugar, beer and tobacco. Or again, if it were to diminish the necessity to reduce wages or had the effect of increasing employment at the existing wage, its effect on working-class standards would probably be favourable. We think that a scheme could be devised which would have no adverse effects on working-class standards.

43. Since many of the arguments in favour of a restriction of imports apply equally in favour of schemes of assistance to exports, some system of restricting imports, accompanied by a policy of giving advantages to the export industries, would seem to be the most practical plan of action.

44. Finally, the immediate effect of such measures in reviving business confidence and a spirit of enterprise scarcely needs to be emphasised.

45. For these reasons and also because relief would be given both to the Budget and to the balance of trade, it would seem that restrictions on imports and aids to exports would run well in double harness with the other class of remedy which we next discuss, namely, schemes of capital development. For it is obvious that the whole of the resources required for capital development at home are necessarily found within the country and as a result of our own efforts and sacrifices, except in so far as their effect is to diminish our net foreign surplus, whether by decreasing our exports or increasing our imports. Thus the "burden" of such schemes, for which we need to make special provision is exactly measured by the burden on the balance of trade. If, therefore, we were to expand investment at home *and* control imports, we should get the favourable effects of both schemes on domestic employment and avoid the disturbing effects of both on our

international balance. *Report of the Committee on Finance and Industry*, 1931, pp 199–203

44 Sir Theodore Gregory   Addendum to Report of the Macmillan Committee

The willingness of J. M. Keynes to abandon Free Trade was not shared by all his colleagues on the Macmillan Committee. Another distinguished economist, who was a member, contributed his own addendum (III) in which he argued against the adoption of tariffs. Professor T. E. (now Sir Theodore) Gregory held chairs in economics at London and Manchester Universities, and his specialist advice has been employed in the service of many states, including the Irish Republic, Greece and India, as well as the Dominions of Australia and New Zealand.

Like those of Keynes, however, the arguments adduced by Gregory in this addendum are technical and pragmatic, and again we have moved away from the elements of moral philosophy which were so often interwoven with the economic arguments of the earlier classical school.

The Problem of the Tariff.

15. It has, however, been suggested that a remedy lies within our grasp, which *can* be applied in the short-run, and from which, at any rate in one of its forms, much can be expected. It has been suggested that the imposition of a Customs duty (of say 10 per cent.) upon all imports, accompanied by a subsidy upon all exports (also of 10 per cent.) would (*a*) improve our balance of trade, (*b*) reduce the real burden of *all* the sterling costs of British industry, including fixed charges, (*c*) increase revenue, less, of course, the cost of subsidies. It would be equivalent in its effects upon *home-income* to a devaluation of 10 per cent. in the standard of value, without raising any of the difficulties attendant upon a direct attempt at devaluation. Even if such a tariff policy proved impracticable, import duties could still be imposed, accompanied by aids to the export industries, similar in effect to,

though not identical with, a direct subsidy. It has even been suggested that such a tariff, in the light of our present situation, is the ideal method of securing the optimum distribution of our national resources.

This last point, though of no great practical importance, would, if it were true, be of great scientific interest. I believe it to be invalid. A flat rate of import duty accompanied by a flat rate of subsidy on the f.o.b. value of exports would indeed make conditions even as between the export industries and industries using home-produced materials and domestic labour, and selling in the home-market. But it would *not* make conditions even as between the production of either of these classes of goods and the production of goods intended for home consumption out of im-ported raw materials: nor would it make conditions even be-tween the first two classes of goods and the rendering of services, in so far as those who render services would have to pay more than before for raw materials and equipment without receiving a subsidy. (Are, e.g., ships built of foreign steel but owned by English firms on the British register to receive a subsidy or not?) But this point is of quite subsidiary importance as compared to the other issues raised.

16. It is only as a possible solution of the monetary difficulties associated with the present emergency that I am concerned with this, or indeed any alternative, proposal involving the imposition of duties upon imports. As a suggested method of overcoming disequilibria associated with monetary difficulties the tariff suffers, indeed, from the fact that it is unable to remove the fundamental defect which is complained of, so that, unless it is constantly being adjusted to meet changes in the situation, its use as a monetary instrument is liable to create new difficulties of its own. Moreover, a review of history does not warrant giving the tariff a very high place as a method of relief from monetary distress. But neither *a priori* considerations nor historical example constitute, in our present circumstances, a sufficient answer to the case put forward by some of my colleagues.

I demur, in the first place, to the definition of this expedient as an emergency measure; one which can be dropped without difficulty when the circumstances which called it into existence have passed away. For such a tariff would tend to perpetuate those disparities between British and foreign costs to the existence of which it would, *ex hypothesi*, owe its existence. So long as these disparities lasted, retention of the tariff could and would be urged as a method of defence, but so long as it was hoped that the tariff would remain, there would be no need to make the efforts necessary to overcome the disparities involved. It might, perhaps, be said that some recovery of world prices is to be expected and that, in so far as foreign money-costs rose, the fact would become so patent that a widespread agitation directed to the removal of the duties would follow. But if a rise in world prices is to be seriously hoped for, within a measurable period of time, this very fact would be a decisive reason for avoiding (unless other grounds than the nature of the present emergency can be invoked) any measures which, once imposed, would involve, in the virtue of their very nature, their permanent retention. If a revival of world prices is not to be hoped for, the tariff ceases to be an emergency measure and would become an integral part of the fiscal and economic system of the country: the more certainly, the longer the period of time involved. Moreover, the tariff history of other countries shows with what tenacity a tariff is clung to, even when, to the eyes of impartial spectators, the industries calling it in aid are clearly able to do without its assistance. If the tariff does what it is asked to do during the emergency period, there will be a natural reluctance to part with so valuable an instrument: if it does not, it can be pleaded that failure to achieve success was due to the inadequacy of the tariff protection actually afforded. If the tariff is to be adopted at all, it is likely to be permanent.

But if anticipations in this respect are well-founded it appears impossible to suppose that Parliament and public opinion will be concerned mainly with the monetary (and supposedly temporary) aspect of the proposal. Discussion would turn, and turn rightly, upon the relative merits of the proposal, as compared

M

with possible alternatives, as a permanent instrument of fiscal policy. What is recommended for a special and temporary reason would be attacked and defended on other and more far-reaching grounds altogether.

17. I question, in the second place, whether a tariff would not result in a spurious equilibrium likely to cause a new series of disequilibria in the course of time. In general, the beneficial effects anticipated could only follow if the reduction in real costs were effective. An attempt to adjust the level of costs, especially wage rates, to the effect of a rise in the cost of living, would at once produce new disequilibria. But, apart from its intended effect in assisting British industry to replace competitive imports by British products (which would assist employment) it is claimed for the measure that it would help in reviving business confidence and the "spirit of enterprise". But in order that it should have these effects, it is not enough that it should create a temporary mood of optimism, to be dashed later on by the failure of the tariff to function as it was intended to do. If, as a result of the imposition of tariff duties, a sharp fall in the volume of competing imports takes place, and the volume of foreign investment is not adjusted to the change in the position of the Balance of Payments, gold would flow in freely, to be utilised to serve as the basis of an expansion of credit.

Thus, if the tariff is at all successful in achieving its objects, it seems reasonable to suppose that it would result in a temporary boom in home industries, and that, under these circumstances, a check would be given to foreign investment, at least for the time being. In the early stages of revival, the Central Bank might find it difficult to offset gold imports by sales of securities, for it would then be liable to be attacked for running counter to the policy of the Government of the day in restoring "confidence", and the anticipated effects upon the volume of credit are, therefore not only possible, but, under the circumstances, not improbable.

The money-income of society would thereupon expand: especially if diminishing unemployment and rising prices led to a rise of money wages. Thereupon, at the new level of money-incomes (the tariff being supposed to remain unchanged) a new stimulus to imports and check to exports is brought into being, and a new disequilibrium between domestic and foreign costs is set up: to be followed either by the collapse of the boom or the imposition of a still higher level of tariffs in order to avoid the threatened breakdown of "confidence". I agree that the question can only be answered definitely by a comparison between particular, alternative projects. A slight measure of tariff protection would necessarily have slight effects. But this would apply to the beneficial, as well as to less attractive, consequences to be expected from the imposition of import duties.

18. Thirdly, I believe that the proposal for a tariff upon all imports accompanied by a subsidy upon all exports would prove hopelessly impracticable, and that the effects of any tariff which would be likely to be imposed would differ markedly from those which, it may be held, would follow from a flat rate of import duty accompanied by a flat rate of subsidy. My belief is not based merely upon the circumstance that, if such a flat-rate tariff and subsidy were imposed, it would be met by countervailing anti-dumping duties in foreign countries and that, in order to avoid the danger of the application of such duties, equivalent advantages to the export industries would have to be devised, the subsidy being dropped in favour of such alternatives. I do not think that the technique of tariff-making is so little understood by foreign countries as to make it at all difficult for them to apply special measures against British goods, merely because we would attempt to grant our export trades concealed, instead of open, bounties.

The main object of the proposed tariff is not to collect revenue but to counterbalance the disadvantages of the British level of costs, as well as to keep out part of the existing imports of goods. But I feel that Parliament would not view with any great favour a scheme of tariff legislation which, whilst it would involve, in all probability, very considerable administrative expenses, would not have the advantages of leaving a large additional net revenue in the hands of the State. In combination with a subsidy, which would make an additional volume of exports possible, the revenue aspect of the proposal is hardly worth taking seriously into consideration. But this would diminish the practical attractiveness of the proposal very much.

19. The probability then is that the tariff as introduced would depart from the postulated simplicity of form and purpose contemplated. Though this is not the place to discuss at length the advantages and disadvantages of Protective Tariffs, it is not straying beyond the limits of the permissible to point out that the more complex and elaborate the tariff, the less can be predicted, in the absence of definite knowledge of what the concrete details are, of the effects of a tariff upon the position of the export trades. In considering the effects of the imposition of a tariff upon exports, it is not enough to take account of the direct reactions which might be expected to result, but attention must also be paid to the indirect reactions. Foreign goods excluded from the British market do not simply disappear; they reappear, in the guise of increased foreign competition, in neutral markets. The net increase in employment under all heads which will result from the imposition of tariffs is therefore likely to be smaller, and the damage to the export trades greater, than appears at first sight. The trade of the world as a whole, of course, is not a fixed magnitude, and it by no means follows that in the long run neutral markets will not be in a position to absorb both a greater amount of British goods and of the goods of countries directly competing with ourselves. But if this argument is valid, it is also valid to argue that an increase in the imports of manufactured articles into this country is not inconsistent with an increased demand for domestic products, in the long run, provided the productivity, and therefore the consuming power of the country, continues to increase. *Report of the Committee on Finance and Industry*, 1931, pp 230–34

---

45 J. M. Keynes   Essays in Persuasion
In this essay, Keynes repeated his argument that the adoption

of restrictive devices would help to solve the country's present difficulties. His exposition is clear and attractive.

It is worth stressing, though, that Keynes advocated tariffs and other restrictions as one possible device among others. He thought that the advantages to be derived would be the same as those to be looked for from devaluation, and when devaluation in fact came a little later, Keynes ceased to argue that tariffs were necessary.

---

6. MITIGATION BY TARIFF[1]

(i) *Proposals for a Revenue Tariff*

(March 7, 1931)

Do you think it a paradox that we can continue to increase our capital wealth by adding both to our foreign investments and to our equipment at home, that we can continue to live (most of us) much as usual or better, and support at the same time a vast body of persons in idleness with a dole greater than the income of a man in full employment in most parts of the world—and yet do all this with one quarter of our industrial plant closed down and one quarter of our industrial workers unemployed? It would be not merely a paradox, but an impossibility, if our potential capacity for the creation of wealth were not much greater than it used to be. But this greater capacity does exist. It is to be attributed mainly to three factors—the ever-increasing technical efficiency of our industry (I believe that output per head is 10 per cent greater than it was even so recently as 1924), the greater economic output of women, and the larger proportion of the population which is at the working period of life. The fall in the price of our imports compared with that of our exports

---

[1] [For some months before the collapse of the gold standard it had become obvious that this collapse was becoming inevitable unless special steps were taken to mitigate the gravity of our problem. Somewhat in desperation, I made various suggestions, and, amongst them, a proposal for a Tariff combined, if possible, with a bounty to exports. Mr. Snowden, endowed with more than a normal share of blindness and obstinacy, opposed his negative to all the possible alternatives, until, at last, natural forces took charge and put us out of our misery.]

also helps. The result is that with three-fourths of our industrial capacity we can now produce as much wealth as we could produce with the whole of it a few years ago. But how rich we could be if only we could find some way of employing *four*-fourths of our capacity to-day!

Our trouble is, then, not that we lack the physical means to support a high standard of life, but that we are suffering a breakdown in organisation and in the machinery by which we buy and sell to one another.

There are two reactions to this breakdown. We experience the one or the other according to our temperaments. The one is inspired by a determination to maintain our standards of life by bringing into use our wasted capacity—that is to say, to expand, casting fear and even prudence away. The other, the instinct to contract, is based on the psychology of fear. How reasonable is it to be afraid?

We live in a society organised in such a way that the activity of production depends on the individual business man hoping for a reasonable profit, or at least, to avoid an actual loss. The margin which he requires as his necessary incentive to produce may be a very small proportion of the total value of the product. But take this away from him and the whole process stops. This, unluckily, is just what has happened. The fall of prices relatively to costs, together with the psychological effect of high taxation, has destroyed the necessary incentive to production. This is at the root of our disorganisation. It may be unwise, therefore, to frighten the business man or torment him further. A forward policy is liable to do this. For reasoning by a false analogy from what is prudent for an individual who finds himself in danger of living beyond his means, he is usually, when his nerves are frayed, a supporter, though to his own ultimate disadvantage, of national contraction.

And there is a further reason for nervousness. We are suffering from *international* instability. Notoriously the competitive power of our export trades is diminished by our high standard of life. At the same time the lack of profits in home business inclines the investor to place his money abroad, whilst high taxation exercises a sinister influence in the same direction. Above all, the reluctance of other creditor countries to lend (which is the root-cause of this slump) places too heavy a financial burden on London. These, again, are apparent arguments against a forward policy; for greater activity at home due to increased employment will increase our excess of imports, and Government borrowing may (in their present mood) frighten investors.

Thus the *direct* effect of an expansionist policy must be to cause Government borrowing, to throw some burden on the Budget, and to increase our excess of imports. In every way, therefore— the opponents of such a policy point out—it will aggravate the want of confidence, the burden of taxation, and the international instability which, they believe, are at the bottom of our present troubles.

At this point the opponents of expansion divide into two groups—those who think that we must not only postpone all ideas of expansion, but must positively contract, by which they mean reduce wages and make large economies in the existing expenditure of the Budget, and those who are entirely negative and, like Mr. Snowden, dislike the idea of contraction (interpreted in the above sense) almost as much as they dislike the idea of expansion.

The policy of negation, however, is really the most dangerous of all. For, as time goes by, it becomes increasingly doubtful whether we *can* support our standard of life. With 1,000,000 unemployed we certainly can; with 2,000,000 unemployed we probably can; with 3,000,000 unemployed we probably cannot. Thus the negative policy, by allowing unemployment steadily to increase, must lead in the end to an unanswerable demand for a reduction in our standard of life. If we do nothing long enough, there will in the end be nothing else that we can do.

Unemployment, I must repeat, exists because employers have been deprived of profit. The loss of profit may be due to all sorts of causes. But, short of going over to Communism, there is no possible means of curing unemployment except by restoring to employers a proper margin of profit. There are two ways of doing this—by increasing the *demand* for output, which is the expansionist cure, or by decreasing the *cost* of output, which is the contractionist cure. Both of these try to touch the spot. Which of them is to be preferred?

To decrease the cost of output by reducing wages and curtailing Budget services may indeed increase foreign demand for our goods (unless, which is quite likely, it encourages a similar policy of contraction abroad), but it will probably diminish the domestic demand. The advantages to employers of a *general* reduction of wages are, therefore, not so great as they look. Each employer sees the advantage to himself of a reduction of the wages which he himself pays, and overlooks both the consequences of the reduction of the incomes of his customers and of the reduction of wages which his competitors will enjoy. Anyway, it would certainly lead to social injustice and violent resistance, since it would greatly benefit some classes of income at the expense of others. For these reasons a policy of contraction sufficiently drastic to do any real good may be quite impracticable.

Yet the objections to the expansionist remedy—the instability of our international position, the state of the Budget, and the want of confidence—cannot be thus disposed of. Two years ago there was no need to be frightened. To-day it is a different matter. It would not be wise to frighten the penguins and arouse these frigid creatures to flap away from our shores with their golden eggs inside them. A policy of expansion sufficiently drastic to be useful might drive us off the gold standard. Moreover, two years ago the problem was mainly a British problem; to-day it is mainly international. No domestic cure to-day can be adequate by itself. An international cure is essential; and I see the best hope of remedying the international slump in the leadership of Great Britain. But if Great Britain is to resume leadership, she must be strong and believed to be strong. It is of paramount importance, therefore, to restore full confidence in London. I do not believe that this is difficult; for the real strength of London is being under-estimated to-day by foreign opinion, and the position is ripe for a sudden reversal of sentiment. For these reasons I, who opposed our return to the gold standard and can claim, unfortunately, that my Cassandra utterances have been partly fulfilled, believe that our exchange position should be relentlessly defended to-day, in order, above all, that we may resume the vacant financial leadership of the world, which no one else has the experience or the public spirit to occupy, speaking out of acknowledged strength and not out of weakness.

An advocate of expansion in the interests of domestic employment has cause, therefore, to think twice. I have thought twice, and the following are my conclusions.

I am of the opinion that a policy of expansion, though desirable, is not safe or practicable to-day, unless it is accompanied by other measures which would neutralise its dangers. Let me remind the reader what these dangers are. There is the burden on the trade balance, the burden on the Budget, and the effect on confidence. If the policy of expansion were to justify itself eventually by increasing materially the level of profits and the volume of employment, the net effect on the Budget and on confidence would in the end be favourable and perhaps very favourable. But this might not be the initial effect.

What measures are available to neutralise these dangers? A decision to reform the grave abuses of the dole, and a decision to postpone for the present all new charges on the Budget for social services in order to conserve its resources to meet schemes for the expansion of employment, are advisable and should be taken. But the main decision which seems to me to-day to be absolutely forced on any wise Chancellor of the Exchequer, whatever his beliefs about Protection, is the introduction of a substantial revenue tariff. It is certain that there is no other measure all the immediate consequences of which will be favourable and appropriate. The tariff which I have in mind would include no discriminating protective taxes, but would cover as wide a field as possible at a flat rate or perhaps two flat rates, each applicable to wide categories of goods. Rebates would be allowed in respect of imported material entering into exports, but raw materials, which make up an important proportion of the value of exports, such as wool and cotton, would be exempt. The amount of revenue to be aimed at should be substantial, not less than £50,000,000 and, if possible, £75,000,000. Thus, for example, there might be import duties of 15 per cent on all manufactured and semi-manufactured goods without exception, and of 5 per cent on all food stuffs and certain raw materials, whilst other raw materials would be exempt.[1] I am prepared to maintain that the effect of such duties on the cost of living would be insignificant—no greater than the existing fluctuation between one month and another. Moreover, any conceivable remedy for unemployment will have the effect, and, indeed, will be intended, to raise prices. Equally, the effect on the cost of our exports, after allowing for the rebates which should be calculated on broad and simple lines, would be very small. It should be the declared intention of the Free Trade parties acquiescing in this decision to remove the duties in the event of world prices recovering to the level of 1929.

Compared with any alternative which is open to us, this measure is unique in that it would at the same time relieve the pressing problems of the Budget and restore business confidence. I do not believe that a wise and prudent Budget can be framed to-day without recourse to a revenue tariff. But this is not its only advantage. In so far as it leads to the substitution of home-produced goods for goods previously imported, it will increase employment in this country. At the same time, by relieving the pressure on the balance of trade it will provide a much-needed margin to pay for the additional imports which a policy of expansion will require and to finance loans by London to necessitous debtor countries. In these ways, the buying power which we take away from the rest of the world by restricting certain imports we shall restore to it with the other hand. Some fanatical Free Traders might allege that the adverse effect of import

---

[1] [In a subsequent article I agreed that this precise scale of duties could not be relied on to produce so large a revenue as that suggested above, and that £40,000,000 was a safer estimate.]

duties on our exports would neutralise all this; but it would not be true.

Free Traders may, consistently with their faith, regard a revenue tariff as our iron ration, which can be used once only in emergency. The emergency has arrived. Under cover of the breathing space and the margin of financial strength thus afforded us, we could frame a policy and a plan, both domestic and international, for marching to the assault against the spirit of contractionism and fear.

If, on the other hand, Free Traders reject these counsels of expediency, the certain result will be to break the present Government and to substitute for it, in the confusion of a Crisis of Confidence, a Cabinet pledged to a full protectionist programme. J. M. Keynes. *Essays in Persuasion*, London, 1931.

Suggestions for Further Reading

Many aspects of the free-trade question have been well covered in recent books. The object of this appendix is to suggest a short list of books and articles which provide a fuller background for the documents cited in this volume.

Of the many histories of economic thought a particularly useful one is M. Blaug's *Economic Theory in Retrospect*. Although this book covers a much wider field than just Free Trade, it contains a perceptive evaluation and criticism of the major economists on the subject. It discusses their arguments and, for most of them, summarises their major works. A somewhat simpler exposition of the same general nature is Eric Roll's *A History of Economic Thought*, which again covers a much wider field but provides sound accounts of the major figures concerned with Free Trade. For a general background to the economic history Sir John Clapham's *An Economic History of Modern Britain*, and S. G. Checkland's *The Rise of Industrial Society in England, 1815–1885*, are useful accounts.

The most recent book on Adam Smith is C. R. Fay's *Adam Smith and the Scotland of his Day*, while there is a good deal of contemporary material on Smith in the older *Adam Smith as Student and Professor*, by W. R. Scott. John W. Derry's *William Pitt, the Younger* is a recent short biography of that statesman.* We have not as yet any good study of Peel's career in full, though this gap is likely to be filled speedily. Norman Gash's *Mr.*

---

* Since the above selection of sources was made the appearance of John Ehrman's *William Pitt* (1969) has given a much fuller treatment of that statesman's career than the short biography by J. W. Derry already mentioned here.

Secretary Peel is a very thorough and perceptive study of Peel's life to 1830, while Dr Kitson Clark's *Peel and the Conservative Party* is another biographical work of note.

The conflict over the Corn Laws in the 1840s has been dealt with by a number of recent works. The most recent treatment of the Anti-Corn Law League at length is N. McCord's *The Anti-Corn Law League*, and the same author has contributed a paper on *Cobden and Bright in Politics, 1846–1857* to a volume of essays in honour of Dr Kitson Clark, *Ideas and Institutions of Victorian Britain*, edited by Robert Robson. The part played by officials of the Board of Trade is discussed by Lucy Brown in *The Board of Trade and the Free-trade Question, 1830–42*. Dr Brown also discussed 'The Chartists and the League', in the volume of *Chartist Studies*, edited by Asa Briggs. The most recent biography of the two apostles of free trade is *Cobden and Bright: A Victorian Political Partnership*, by Donald Read. Though not primarily concerned with economic questions, this book is now the most convenient account of the lives of these two men. A book devoted more to exposition of the arguments adduced by the free traders is *The Manchester School of Economics*, by W. D. Grampp. Robert Blake's *Disraeli* has much to say of the opposition to Peel in 1846 and the subsequent abandonment of protection by the Conservatives.

The best account of the early moves against Free Trade is *The Tariff Reform Movement in Great Britain 1881–1895*, by B. H. Brown. A cautionary word is needed here: this book has many merits, but it is important in using it to remember that in these years tariff reform did not occupy the centre of the political stage in Britain. For Chamberlain's campaign for tariff reform a very full account is given in *Joseph Chamberlain & the Tariff Reform* which takes up the last two volumes (V and VI) of the major life of Chamberlain recently completed by Julian Amery. This coverage amounts to more than 1,000 pages; a much more succinct account, but necessarily slighter, is provided by the relevant section of Peter Fraser's *Joseph Chamberlain*. L. S. Amery's *My Political Life* provides a readable account of the tariff-reform crusade by one who was active in it, and the fervent imperialism enunciated there again shows how far the question of Free Trade was from being merely an academic argument on economics. Roy Jenkins's *Asquith* gives an account of the tariff reform battle from the other side of the political fence.

The Life of John Maynard Keynes, by R. F. Harrod, and the more recent *The Age of Keynes* by R. Lekachman, cover that major figure. The fullest account of the 1931 crisis, which led to the abandonment of Free Trade, is given in *1931—Political Crisis* by R. Bassett. *A History of British Tariffs 1913–1942*, by D. Abel, and R. K. Snyder's *Tariff Problems in Great Britain 1918–1933*, are more technical accounts of the tariff problem in the present century.

One aspect of the history of Free Trade merits special attention, for it is currently a subject of contention among historians, and has not yet produced any agreement. This is the extent to which British policy after the formal adoption of Free Trade paid anything more than lip-service to the Cobdenite ideals of non-intervention by government in commercial matters. The issue is whether or not British governments were still pursuing a deliberate policy of economic imperialism in the period after 1846 and the adoption of Free Trade. The debate was inaugurated by an important paper from J. Gallagher and R. E. Robinson, 'The Imperialism of Free Trade', in *Economic History Review*, VI, No 1, 1953. The arguments adduced there were expanded further in a book by the same authors, *Africa and the Victorians*. A more traditional view was expounded by Oliver MacDonagh, 'The Anti-Imperialism of Free Trade', in *Ec Hist Rev*, XIV, No 3, 1962. On the whole the arguments for the imperialism of Free Trade have not fared as well as the more old-fashioned arguments against. An example of analysis in detail to test the rival interpretations is W. M. Mather's 'The Imperialism of Free Trade: Peru, 1820–1870', in *Ec Hist Rev*, XXI, No 3, 1968. The most useful reconsideration of the topic at present is D. C. M. Platt's 'The Imperialism of Free Trade: Some Reservations', in *Ec Hist Rev*, XXI, No 2, 1968.

Index